The Happiness Handbook

Lessons from My Father and Beyond

Divyam Gupta

Title   :   The Happiness Handbook : Lessons from My Father
               and Beyond

Author   :   Divyam Gupta

Edition   :   First (October, 2024)

ISBN   :   9789348037732

Published by

A Venture by -
PRACHI DIGITAL PUBLICATION

Regd. Add.: 254, Khuriyakhatta No. 10, Bindukhatta,
Lalkuan, Nainital - 262402, Uttarakhand, India
Website : www.taneeshapublishers.in
E-mail : taneeshapublishers@gmail.com
Phone : +91 845481 2712, +91 976041 7980

Printed by :

Manipal Technologies Limited, Bengaluru - 560001, Karnataka

INDEX

Acknowledgements

- I begin by offering my deepest gratitude to Kanhaji, whose divine presence and blessings have been my guiding light throughout this journey.

- I extend my heartfelt thanks to My Spiritual Guru, whose teachings have profoundly shaped my understanding of happiness and life's purpose.

- A special thanks to My Grandparents—Rakesh, Archana, Satish, and Santosh. Your love, wisdom, and guidance have been the cornerstone of my life and the inspiration behind this book.

- To my parents, Vaibhav and Kavita, who have instilled in me the values and lessons that form the foundation of this book, I am forever grateful. Your unwavering support and belief in me have been the driving force.

- My sincere thanks to My Uncle and Aunts—Gaurav, Nidhi, Saras, Megha, Ashish, and Shreya. Your encouragement and affection have been a source of strength and comfort.

- To My Brother and Sisters—Naman, Yashvi, Samaika, and Rimaya, thank you for the joy, love, and inspiration you bring into my life each day.

- I am also deeply grateful to My Friends—Rakshan, Ashvath, and Sambhav. Your friendship and support have added immeasurable value to my life and to this work.

- Finally, I express my sincere appreciation to My Teachers, Mentors, and Coaches. Your guidance, wisdom, and dedication have played a crucial role in my personal and intellectual growth. Thank you for helping me become who I am today.

- This book is a reflection of the love, wisdom, and happiness that each of you has contributed to my life. I am deeply thankful for your presence and support.

Preface

This book is my way to share with the reader the valuable lessons that my father imparted to me about happiness, perseverance, and self-acceptance. Being a typical Indian child, I was also taught that happiness is not something one goes out chasing; it is something one decides to experience every day. My father taught me about family and people who surround you and the beauty of small things in life. This book is the result of looking at the pearls of lessons that I have embraced to expect the same from you; to embrace the joy in every instance of your life and gain true happiness while nurturing a sustainable inner peace.

Author's Note

This book is a tribute to my father, whose values and words influenced the perception of happiness in my life. From what I learnt in his teachings, it is clear that happiness is achieved in the smallest things that we get to experience in life, in having a thankful attitude, and in overcoming sorrow. The insights he taught people—from thinking positively to valuing community—are as crucial today as yesterday and as close to the expert's heart as in the best days of his practice. It is my hope that this work will be of assistance and motivation to anyone who is searching for happiness and dignity. I would like the readers to take note of the fact that happiness is not a destination but rather a journey that is embraced by self-acceptance of oneself, acceptance of others, and leading a life that has significance.

My father coming from a typical Indian background made it a point to remind me that happiness is something one practices and is not something out of reach or a dream that cannot be attained. His book "Happiness: How, When & Why" has impacted my perspective to learn to respect and value my family, care about the community, and accept myself. These values based on Indian culture and spiritual beliefs form the ground upon which I have developed my own belief system. Thus, when writing this, it is my hope to impart these principles to others, both adolescents and adults, who can gain hope and strength just as I did from my father's advice. It is my hope that you will be able to locate your source of joy in this book.

Introduction: The Way of Happiness

Happiness is a relative concept that is debated by academics, thinkers from many fields, and regular people. To me, happiness is not an idea or even a dream; it's a real thing that I can achieve. As a seventeen-year-old Indian boy, many things in my life, including the influence of my father's advice, make this clear. My father wrote a book called "Happiness: How, When & Why." He was an amazing person with a warm heart and a mind full of knowledge. For me, this book helped me get through the tough parts of being a teenager and figure out what true happiness is.

Due to my heritage and that I came from a traditional Indian home, my father was not only my parent, but also my teacher, counsellor, and friend. In a city that was constantly changing, this meant that people's homes became places where they could learn and fall in love. My father's study, which was full of different kinds of books, was the place I wanted to be. That's where I first found my dad's book on happiness, among the dust, the smell of books, and the noise of the ceiling fan.

The First Encounter

Yes, I do remember the incident very clearly. It was a monsoon evening and it was raining hard, there was a soft melody of dripping water on the tin roof. One day, while I was actually searching for something to do so that I would not be bored, I chanced upon a book written by my father. Externally, it had a plain and somewhat austere-looking cover but it radiated a certain kind of homeliness. "Happiness:

How, When & Why" I, therefore, took it and began to read It. It is rather paradoxical that sooner than I thought, this book became a significant part of my life.

It was a very personal item, something that contained not only words but my father's soul. Every chapter reflected his observations, his feelings and his wise words. The words he was saying were as if he was telling to me, his principles for making life happier. I remember he was effusively talking and ended his last message in a way that made me feel his presence, his love, his support and his hope for happiness.

Lessons Learned

The first lesson my father gave in his book was the element of gratitude, its significance, and necessity. He often described how gratitude changes life, and how it can enable one to change perspective from lack to abundance. When I read those lines, I thought too of all the times that my father has told me to be grateful for what I have and for what I have received. The words he did have to say were life-changing, and I started incorporating gratitude into my day more actively.

One of the most important things that was taught was the importance of positive thinking. What my father was trying to tell me was that we presuppose what we see, or as he used to put it; the way we think defines the reality around us. He often repeated words like "what we think, we become". This book particularly focused on having a favourable perspective towards life or any situation in life. I can genuinely say that this lesson proved to be highly useful during my examination period in which pressure and tension generally affect my thoughts. Following my father's advice, I attempted to accentuate the positives and this improved my morale and produced better results.

The Influence of Culture

My father, being an Indian, had his own set of beliefs imbibed strongly in Indian culture. In most of his discourses, he likes to relate the idea of happiness to facets of old Indian wisdom and principles. In his book, he also explained the royal path of the Bhagavad Gita based on the principles of selfless work and morality. He also expounded on how one attains the state of happiness, which is not the pursuit of one's interests but the performance of duties.

This amplified my understanding of his teachings because I could relate them to what happens in our society's culture. Whether it was the festivals that we were celebrating, the family gatherings that we enjoyed, or the acts of kindness that we performed, I came to realise how much of our culture was based on the belief in happiness and its attainment.

Personal Anecdotes

His examples were real-life situations which he narrated in his book thus making the stories very convincing. He was sharing experiences, focusing on his youth and what it was like to have simple childhood vices. These stories were to some degree, or rather in their simplicity, themselves educational, showing me that money does not guarantee happiness, and that true greatness is in trivia.

The other story he narrated to me from his book that left a big influence on me was regarding family functions. My father related how in spite of various activities, commitments and engagements taken by his parents they ensured that the family sat together. These personal experiences, aside from being mere recollections, were life's positive and freshness found in the ordinariness. They ensured that I learned that there can be happiness in even the simplest forms, be it in a good laugh, a created object or, the embrace of the family. His life taught me that success does not lie in what people own but in how they view the world and the bonds that are cultivated. This anecdote made me understand that it is not about utter failure but the family support and the strength to struggle.

Considering these stories, I realised that happiness can be found in one's own life by paying attention to those minor occurrences and the people in one's life My father gifted me the ability to find happiness in the mundane and the relationships in our lives. His tales are good-natured and underline the fact that real happiness comes from within and that there is happiness to be had in all sorts of commonplace things.

A Guiding Light

During the difficult and thus not always easy teenage years, the book penned by my father really helped me to understand many things. This was a book in which I always took solace whenever I found myself confused or stuck. It was like talking to my father even when such a personality was not around. Thanks to him and his powerful words, I knew I had the strength and courage to face all my fears and finally chase my dreams.

That one of the strongest points he made in his book was the one about acceptance of oneself was a very strong one. My father also stressed the need to embrace one's self despite our flaws. He added that true happiness is internal happiness, the happiness that comes along with the inner sense of self-acceptance. I can relate to this message each time whenever I feel that I am not capable of doing something or whenever am in fear. His words made me understand how important it is to love myself accept myself with my strengths and weaknesses and know that I deserve the best.

The Impact on My Relationships

Families also influenced my development, with my father's teachings impacting my relationships more than my other characters. His book underlined that love, compassion, and empathy are the foundations of a healthy and warm relationship. He narrated how happy people are happier when with others, and how positive energy generates more when passed on in the form of kindness and tolerance.

I attempted to use these principles in my interactions with family and friends as he motivated me. I was taught to be a better listener, to acknowledge other people's problems and try to help them; to 'never give up'. Not only did it help build these relations, but for me personally, it also became a source of pleasure and satisfaction. The happily transformed faces and expressions of people to whom I offered my care lifted my spirit and strengthened my belief that love and compassion indeed move the world.

A Vision for the Future

Looking at the future, I am full of hope and I am very much excited as I plan my future. Drawing from my father's book, I have learned key things in life including forming the fundamental groundwork of what happiness should be. It has enlightened me as to the fact that happiness is not really stated but rather, a process and a state of being which needs to be constantly worked upon and for which we need to remain conscious. It has taught me that the most profound type of happiness is derived from being genuine and accepting what is.

It is my intention to continue the lessons my father passed down to me, the good-natured lessons I want to impart to everyone else. His book, "Happiness: "How, When and Why,"' is not just a guide to happiness but a homage to his love, his wisdom and the very spirit of a man who dedicated his life to the concept of happiness. It is a gift I will treasure till tomorrow, the next and every other day of my life.

Thus, the most important notion related to happiness that I have ever received from my father is the choice I made based on his teachings. I always found guidance, strength, and comfort in his book to face adolescent hardship with dignity and success. Alas, I move on, thankful for the lessons he has taught me and for the love he gave me His words made me the person I am now, and for that, I vow to spend my remaining years spreading the lessons he taught me about happiness.

Chapter 1

Wisdom from the Elders

Importance of respecting and learning from the wisdom of elders

The things I learned from my ancestors, especially my father, are still some of the most important and weighty ways of thinking that have shaped how I think about happiness. Happiness: How, When, and Why, his book, helped people find a way to live a rich life. Here, I'll talk about the important things I've learned from my father and other older people, with a focus on how their advice has shaped my ideas about happiness.

In Indian society, honour and wisdom are very important, especially when it comes to family and older people. People think of elders as knowledgeable people and ask them for advice on a wide range of life problems. In spite of this, my dad lived by this concept in both his book and his everyday life. He used to tell me stories from his life, and those little events were full of lessons that showed me that life doesn't teach us values or lessons; it shapes us through our experiences and reminds us that happiness doesn't come from material things but from the little things that happen in life and the bonds that hold us together.

The most important thing my dad taught me was that everyone should love and accept themselves. During his speech, he tried to explain the idea of happiness that doesn't always come from what we've accomplished or from being liked by others. This really helped me understand why I was having so much trouble as a teen, like not having enough confidence and the pressure from my peers. Father told me to stay true to myself and be content with who I am, not to worry about what other people think of me or what I own.

When my dad talked about his youth, I loved hearing about how he and his friends of the same age were able to make the most of what they had. He grew up in a world that wasn't very advanced technologically. He didn't grow up with all the technological advances that people do today. He could go into great detail about how many days he spent with friends, how nice it was to eat with his family, or how good it felt to lend a hand. Simple lessons about how to live a happy life in the present with what little you have were told through these stories.

Besides the Holi story, there was another fun story for kids about a holiday he remembered from his own childhood. He talked about the happy sounds, bright colours, and a sense of community that spread through the whole neighbourhood. What really struck me about him, though, was how happy and content he seemed to be when he was with his family, celebrating different occasions and spending time with people he cared about. The main point of this story is that people are happiest when they are with their friends and in the relationships they build.

Another important thing my dad knew was how to help people be patient and positive about life. His favourite words were, Life is an ebb and flow, and man's character determines whether he is happy or unhappy. He taught me that problems should not be seen as problems but as opportunities to grow. He also told me to always look on the good side of things, no matter what. The bravery and happiness in his words give me strength. They don't mean that there won't be problems, but they will help me face them with pride and hope.

The idea of constant beta and the need to always learn and ask questions was also emphasised in my dad's book. He believed that the only way to be truly happy was to study and learn about oneself all the way through life. I remember that this lesson had a big effect on how I planned for the future as I went on. Some of the things he told me were that I should set personal goals, be curious, and never stop learning. In addition to helping me do better in school, it also made me feel like I had accomplished something and was meant to do something.

Being around older people in my family, like my grandparents or teachers, who have more life experience than I do, like my father, also shaped how I see happiness. The action scenes also showed how the main characters changed and how they accepted personal-change ideals like being humble, appreciating what they have, and caring about other people. I learned that being happy isn't just being happy with yourself; it's also helping other people and making their lives better. These older people had a big impact on my personality and helped me really understand what other people were saying.

The first people who come to mind when I think about happiness and the things that may have shaped how I see it are my grandparents. They have been through a lot of hard times, but they have always been strong and had a good attitude. A lot of what they told me was about how they dealt with and got through hard times. This taught me that happiness is not the lack of problems, but a way of handling them. I learned some lessons about faith and hope from them before they were pushed to the point where the spirit rebels and says, "You are happy whether you want to be or not."

The adults also had an effect on how I felt about belonging to a group and making friends. From what my dad and other older people have told me, living with other people brings happiness. They helped me build good conversation and relationship skills, as well as the kind of understanding, friendly, and respectable personality that is expected in today's world. I cannot stress enough how important these lessons were in teaching me that my happiness is closely linked to the happiness of others and that making others happy makes us happy as well.

When I think about these things, it's been great to have older people teach me what I need to know. In more than one way, their ideas about acceptance, persistence, learning, and getting along with others have changed how I think about what it means to be happy. Happiness: How, When, & Why, my dad's book, is a true story of those timeless rules that can help anyone live a happy, full life.

After looking at this, it's clear that the custom that lies in the wise words of the elders is in how my father helped me see happiness. Their stories, experiences, and advice are interesting, useful, and helpful. They helped me understand that happiness is inside, in moments, in strength, in friendships, in learning new things all the time, and in experiences. The things I've learned and thoughts I've had about this subject have been important and useful all through my life.

Traditional Indian values and their role in happiness

Since my parents are Indian, some traditional Indian ideas about happiness have also influenced how I feel about myself. My dad's book "Happiness: How, When, & Why" has been helpful and educational. He has taught me the importance of these ideals and how they translate into a meaningful life. Like many teenage boys, I've learned about the deep-seated philosophy in our society and how it can help people figure out how to be happy and deal with life's problems.

Brave Indian ideals include respecting elders, being humble, being thankful, and working together to make peace. It's not just an idea that these ideals exist; they're part of everyday life. I learned as a child to always listen to and follow the advice of my teachers, who are seen as the best sources of information and knowledge. Parents and grandparents played a big part in my dad's life. They taught him important lessons that helped him become a good person and find happiness.

The importance of family was one that my dad always talked about. It might have been the most important one. There is an Indian custom that says happiness and comfort come from family. People in Indian homes live close to each other, which makes them feel safe and close. My dad's book has pictures and words about him, his siblings, and his mom. The pictures and words show that family relationships are truly blessed. Happiness can come from simple things in life, like being able to enjoy holidays with family and friends and being able to stick together during tough times.

Being respectful of older people is another traditional value that my dad brought up. People hold their ancestors in high regard because they knew a lot and were well-known in the community. I remember my dad telling me that his parents and grandparents taught him a lot about life through their stories and words of wisdom. They helped him understand what it means to be humble, patient, and persistent. And those are the things I learned, which is why I still believe that learning from older people is valuable.

Politeness and humility are also important parts of Indian society. The Indian people are also known for being very grateful. In his book, my dad also wrote about how important it is to be humble and appreciate what you have. He believed that being humble was the best way to learn and that being thankful was the best way to accept life as it is and enjoy all the good things in it. Keeping these values close to my heart has helped me stay humble and always be thankful for what I have.

Another traditional Indian value that my father was very excited about was keeping the balance within and finding inner peace. There was a lot of talk in the book about how happiness is an internal state or attitude that has little to do with what happens to other people. Meditation, yoga, and awareness are all things that Indians do, and they are thought to help people become more calm. These habits were part of my dad's daily routine, and he would sometimes tell me to work them out too. He said that by training your mind to be calm, you can handle everything that comes your way in life and be happy as a result.

He also stressed the importance of being thrifty and happy with what one has in their home. It came out at a time when people thought they could find happiness by getting more money. His book was a gentle wake-up call for people to find happiness in simple things and be happy with what they have. He sometimes talked about his childhood, which made me think that he was very happy when he talked to people, played with friends, was outside, or did artistic things. These stories taught me that how much someone owns something doesn't matter as much as how much they enjoy using it.

As a child, my father taught me morals that I try to teach my own children. Being kind and helping others is without a question one of the best things you could inherit. In India, family traditions are closely linked to ideals that are good for society. Being involved in community service was something my dad taught me was important because he did it all the time. He used to say that when we help others and care about their well-being, we make them happy and subsequently feel happy ourselves.

This is another thing my dad always told me: never give up, no matter what. It all depends on how strong you are when you face problems in life. He loved writing in his book about the times he kept his cool and kept going through hard times. These stories moved me, which made me think that bad luck only lasts for a short time and that anyone can change their life and be happy no matter what.

Another thing my dad taught me was how important it is to keep learning. Education is an important part of Indian culture because it is seen as a way to make people and society stronger. That information is a powerful tool that can help you have a good life and be successful, as he always said. He told them to be interested, learn as much as they could, and try not to get too comfy. Following this value has helped me get good grades in school and keep wanting to learn for a long time.

Thinking about these traditional Indian beliefs and what my father taught me, I think they have had a big effect on how I see happiness. It guides me in life and gives me the strength to deal with problems politely and with hope. I learned from them that happiness is in the heart, in friendships, in the little things in life, and in the never-ending search for unity and self-improvement.

Finally, the traditional Indian values that my dad taught me through his book "Happiness: How, When, & Why" have made a big difference in how I think about happiness. Family, respecting older people, being humble, being thankful, finding inner peace, being frugal, having empathy, being patient, and always wanting to learn and get better are some of the values that everyone should follow to live a happy and fulfilling life. These are the lessons I will carry with me on this journey, and I am so grateful to those who have gone before me for how much they have taught me.

Chapter 2

The Role of Family in Happiness

The significance of joint families and strong familial bonds

An important part of Indian culture is the idea of joint families. This is one of the main ideals that has shaped how I see happiness. The lessons my dad taught me in his book "Happiness: How, When, & Why" have shaped my family's view, especially the idea of living with my parents. As an Indian teenager, I've learned that close family ties bring a lot of happiness, safety, and a sense of success that makes life beautiful.

In India, joint families have been around for a long time. In these homes, everyone lives together. My dad always talked about how happy and close that family used to be. He talked about how the space with grandparents, uncles, aunts, and cousins was active and made for a good atmosphere. Growing up in a joint family was a great way to learn and gain knowledge. I have personally felt this sense of community and connection, and it's something I hold dear.

That there is no feeling of fear in a joint family is another thing that I remember my father talking about a lot. No one in a joint family is ever left to deal with a problem on their own. Every time you need help, support, or just someone to listen, there is always someone there. Some of the stories in my dad's book about his life showed how his family helped him through hard times. At that time, the family was there to help each other when there were money troubles, illnesses, or depression. This steady support is one of the most important things that leads to happiness and health.

Sharing experiences with others can make you happy, and shared families are no different. The stories my dad told me most of the time were about how happy he was on holidays, birthdays, and other special days. These events weren't just things that different family members did well; they were times when everyone came together. A feeling of happiness came from the careful planning, planned charisma of the event, and unity of the crowd. These memories come back to me when my whole family celebrates the festivals of light and colour, Diwali and Holi, by eating a big meal together. Those are the times that we will always remember and that will make us stronger in love and happiness.

In Indian families, especially mixed families, putting a lot of value on the older members is held in high regard. In my dad's book, he always talked about how important it was to get help and advice from grandparents. Young people should respect their parents and see their words, ideas, and actions as lessons for the next generation. After watching the movie and listening to the record, I learned it's good to take my grandparents' advice. Sharing their own life situations and going through their happiness and sadness is very helpful and makes them feel more grounded. This is how my elders treat me, and the knowledge passed down from generation to generation in a shared family makes me very happy.

Every person in a joint family has some kind of duty to take care of the family, which is another important thing that my dad told me. A mixed family is one where many people work together to get things done. This way, the work is spread out among many people. When people are responsible for something, they work together and become very united, which keeps teams and groups together. Regarding how everyone was involved, my dad's baby rhymes always had everyone in the family involved, from the little kids to the adults. This not only made daily tasks go more quickly, but it also taught people how to work together and respect each other's wants and manners. Believing that we are all part of the same team makes us happier because it gives us a good view of life.

Joint families are great because they help each other feel better. In his book, my dad often wrote about times when family members were there for each other through good times and bad. This is because life is better when you have a big family to share the good and bad times with. Feeling emotionally connected can help lower stress and give you a sense of safety. For me, trusting that my family will be there for me makes me feel good about my skills. It helps me remember that love is always there for me, no matter how bad things get or how lonely I feel.

The most important thing my dad taught me is how to be flexible and willing to settle when living with other people in the same family. There are a lot of different personalities, tastes, and points of view in one house when you stay with a lot of different people. In the stories, my dad told me, the problems and how they were fixed came up a lot. I think these events made me understand how important it is to be tolerant, understanding, and flexible for everyone's sake. People should learn how to fit in with their neighbours and with other people in society. This will make them happy as individuals.

In addition, my dad believed that joint families were the best way to pass on cultures and traditions. The rules, values, traditions, and customs of joint family systems are the same and are followed by everyone. Our strong and positive connection to our culture and traditions can grow stronger when we all take part in cultural events together. In his book, my dad wrote about some ancient ceremonies and festivals that help keep our culture alive. Being in a home that values its culture so much has helped me accept my roots and feel whole as a person.

As my dad talked about, another thing is that mixed families are financially stable. One of the benefits of living with other people is being able to share resources, which is especially helpful when money is tight. Some of the things my dad told me were about how the family took care of each other by helping each other out financially. This shared financial security takes away people's worries and makes them feel safe and content. We feel safe and protected because we know that our family will be there for us when things get tough.

As a result, one of the most important things my dad taught me was the value of joint families and close relationships. He also taught me that happiness should be a meaningful goal. Respecting elders, sharing duty, emotional support, compromise, cultural values, and financial security are all important parts of the idea of a joint family system that will be talked about more in this paper. Because of these beliefs, the kids will be raised in a caring place where they feel safe, loved, and at home. As I go on my own trip, I carry with me memories and stories from my family's past. I know that our ties to each other and to past generations are the only things that can make us happy.

Stories and lessons from my family

As a child in an Indian home, the stories and lessons in my dad's book "Happiness: How, When, & Why" changed the way I think about what it means to be happy. During my teenage years, my dad's words about family, love, and support have been a lighthouse, showing me how important it is for family members to be close.

As far back as I can remember, family was the most important thing in my life. We are lucky to live in a house where laughing and the excitement of everyday life can be heard everywhere. When my dad was young, he loved to tell stories about how family is what makes you happy and strong. His stories weren't just retellings of events that happened in the past; they were also deep metaphors that changed the way I thought and behaved.

People around me and my dad would often hear stories from his childhood about Sundays. In contrast to today's digitalized weekends, his Sundays were simple yet jam-packed with joy. The man in question would be happy and look forward to the day's events when he woke up. Early in the morning, his family would get up and make a big breakfast together. Everyone would help in some way. In those days, my dad, who was still a little boy, would help his mum make the best roti in the kitchen. With the sound of people talking and laughing and the smell of food, the kitchen became a sign of unity and happiness. Cooking and eating taught him about having to take care of things and the joy of having a family.

These stories taught me that happiness is found in the little things that happen every day. I learned to enjoy our family dinners because I wanted to be like my dad, who loved them. With everything going on in the world, we made dinner time a special time of the day. In this setting, people would gather around the table and talk about their days. Even though they were simple and every day, these times told us that we are strong as a family.

The precious lesson the father told was about being kind to others, which is related to being able to help people through spiritual ups and downs. It was always shown that as a family, they would always be there for each other when they were weak. One story that I still remember very clearly is about how they had monetary trouble when he was a teenager. My dad told me that they saw hard times as times that bring people together, not as times that break the family spirit. So, they learned to rely on each other, to lean on each other when things got tough, and to understand that they were stronger together.

This story taught me that a man's power comes from his family's support. For me, being happy doesn't mean having no problems. It means being able to deal with them while having someone by your side. The above lesson gives me strength every time I'm having a hard time in my own life. I know that my family will always be there for me, which is why I can handle hard times with a smile.

Fun things to do and celebrations were other things my dad liked to talk about. He often talked about how his family turned an event into a party on its own, especially during holidays. This kind of holiday can be seen in Diwali, which means "festival of lights." My dad told me a lot of stories about Diwali. He remembers the diyas, rangoli, sweets, and a lot more very well. But what stood out more than the parties was how friendly everyone was. Festivals like Diwali were a way for families to come together, no matter what colour they were or something like that. The joy of these parties didn't come from having a lot of money, but from being with other people and feeling loved.

When we read stories like these, it makes us feel like Diwali is more like home, which makes us love it more. That is, it wasn't just a desire for the rituals; it was also a chance to help strengthen family bonds. A group of us would get together to clean the house, put up lights, and make holiday-themed food. Many of the things we did above were very easy, but they made us happy and reminded us how important family is to us.

I also heard my dad talk about the wise words his grandparents taught him and how important it is for older people to teach younger ones. Many times, he talked about how his grandpa used to read him stories from the Mahabharata and Ramayana and teach him morals, bravery, and kindness. Not only were they fun, but they also taught him things, and they helped shape his character as a child. He was able to learn from his grandparents and took the lessons of perseverance to do things right regardless of the fate waiting for them.

I respect my grandparents even more now that I've been reading about old wise sayings. So, their stories and experiences became things I could learn from, and I found that their years of life had taught me a lot about how to live and what happiness means. That is why I had to engage in conversation with them, hear their experiences, and follow their counsel to understand what it is to be happy.

Along with personal stories, my dad's book also stressed how important it is for family members to talk to each other. He believed that people should be able to get together, talk about problems, and then decide what to do. He thought it was funny that his four-person family would probably get together and talk about their problems. That way, everyone could say how they feel. Not only were they able to talk about their problems, but it also made their relationship better.

Going forward, I made an effort to tell the truth to my family more often. Someone I knew could help me if I was having trouble or didn't understand something. The things they said to me were never meant to put me down. Instead, they were meant to help me deal with problems and boost my confidence. I could share things with my friends because of this part of the open conversation. It made me feel important and happy.

In addition, my dad insisted that everyone in the family should love and honour each other. He talked a lot about how much his parents loved and respected each other and how they loved each other. This made everyone appreciate how much everyone else loved and cared for them. The love and respect they got in that home were all that important to them.

Therefore, I made sure I loved and respected my family. It crept into my words and actions that I was being kind and grateful, as well as showing understanding and everyday courtesy. These small acts of kindness brought us closer together and made the house a happy place to be. The lessons and stories in my dad's book "Happiness: How, When, & Why," have had a big impact on how I think about happiness. The ideals I hold dear are joint families, happy times together, family support, elders' knowledge, freedom of speech, love, and respect. These beliefs have always been a part of being an Indian teen, and they have taught me that family is the key to happiness.

Chapter 3

Embracing Spirituality

How spirituality and religious practices contribute to happiness

Religion and philosophy have always been important to my family, and my father, Vaibhav Gupta, taught me a lot about them. According to my dad's book "Happiness: How, When, & Why," faith and religious activities can help people be happy. As a teen, I lived in India and was part of a culture where religion is a big part of everyday life.

For as long as I can remember, I've watched my dad do yoga and meditate every morning. He was known to have said things like, "Self-contentment is essential to happiness," which means that externals don't make you stable. Being around this man made me realise that spirituality isn't about following rules and rituals, but about the person and their surroundings. This link brings back happiness and lessens the stress and fear of daily life.

My dad taught me that it's important to follow different ways of life. Mindfulness and how being in the present moment could make me happy were new ideas he taught me. He often talked about the words "Action in hands, quietness in heart," which come from Sri Sri Ravi Shankar. This probably made me aware of things I wouldn't have otherwise, like how much I loved spending time with my family or in the morning. That made me feel more stable and ready to move on with my life.

Another important part of our faith was prayer. One thing our family did was sit and say a prayer for a few minutes every night before bed. The way my dad saw it, prayer was all about thanking God and asking for help. "Let the GOD rest next to me" was something he said a lot. You know that GOD is always with us and helps and encourages us in life. At these prayer groups, people didn't just chant prayers. They were also times to get to know each other, talk about our problems, and find comfort in prayer.

My dad also stressed the idea of "sewa," or selfless service. He always told me, "Sewa—मनसा, वाचा, कर्मणा," which means to serve with your thoughts, words, and deeds. He thought that a man would be happy if he gave something with the hope of getting something in return. So, I did other kinds of community service projects after following his lead. It's nice to be able to help other people, like by teaching younger students or volunteering at a local charity. They taught me that the only way to be happy is to make other people's lives better.

In addition to helping us grow in our faith, my dad also wanted us to learn about other faiths. He thought that faith wasn't the only way to be spiritual and that every religion had something good to teach us. He said the words of Mahatma Gandhi, "Be the change that you wish to see in the world," close to each other. This was done to show how important compassion is for peace. I learned that I could accept people of different religions and look for the good in everyone I met.

I think the most useful thing my dad taught me is the idea of upbeat mantras. He thought that the mind makes reality and that promises, which are words, could change how people see things. He would say "I allow, I deserve, I accept" over and over again, which makes people feel good and love themselves. I chose to use themes in my daily life after giving what he said some thought. I felt happy and more hopeful about life when I said these simple words over and over with energy and purpose.

Meditation was another spiritual thing that my dad liked to do. He taught me the basics of different types of meditation, like guided visualisation or deep breathing. He always said, "ज्ञान, योग, धारणा, सेवा" which means "knowledge, yoga, concentration, and service." I learned how to clear my thoughts, focus, and listen to myself by meditating. This practice helped me stay cool and focused, which was important for me as a teenager going through tough times.

The role of nature in religious rituals was also talked about by my dad in his book. Besides that, he strongly believed that doing things outside could help people get closer to God and find peace. He talked a lot about religion and said that nature shows what a person is like. His lessons made me want to spend more time under trees, whether I was walking in the park or just sitting by myself. I felt more connected to the world during these times spent in nature, which gave me ideas and peace.

In his directions, my dad also told us how important it was to forgive and let go of things that hurt or offended us. "The person who serves the best profits the most," he would say to emphasise this point. This meant that people shouldn't hate each other because it doesn't help anyone. One of the most important things I had to learn on my spiritual journey was how to forgive and forget. I was able to let go of all the bad emotions inside me and only accept the good things that happened to me.

In addition to spiritual activities that people did alone, my dad also liked spiritual activities that people did together. He set up a lot of family get-togethers where we talked about spiritual things, shared stories and experiences, and helped each other grow spiritually. People felt better after these kinds of meetings because they reminded them that everyone is linked and can help each other. "Supporting Not Interfering" was something my dad would say. It meant that if you help someone grow, you have to let them do it their way.

The lessons in my dad's book and other leaders' books have had a big impact on how I think about faith. Being able to learn these things at such a young age has made my life more satisfying and joyful. My dad told me that being a lover and a caring person is more important than following the rules.

Based on what my father, Vaibhav Gupta, said, I can say that becoming more spiritual has been a very enlightening experience in my life. "Happiness: How, When, & Why," his book, It's like a map that shows the way to good living and, eventually, real happiness through spiritual practice. Some of these lessons are prayer and meditation, caring about other people, and good self-talk. They have made my life richer and happier. These are some of the spiritual lessons I carry with me as I go through life. I know that these lessons will always lead to a better and more fulfilling life.

The impact of yoga, meditation, and rituals

The faith in my family was very strong, and my father, Vaibhav Gupta, and the lessons he taught from his book "Happiness: How, when, & Why" often moved me. As a child, my father taught me yoga, meditation, and routines that became a way to live a happy spiritual life.

His daily usual exercise was yoga, which he did without fail every day. He thought of yoga as more than just a way to work out. It was a complicated practice that brought the body, mind, and spirit together. He would say that the four things you need to live a balanced life are knowledge, yoga, focus, and service-"ज्ञान, योग, धारणा, सेवा". When I saw that he did different asanas every morning, I knew that yoga was a good way to keep the mind and body healthy. My dad always liked to quote B. K. S. Iyengar: "Yoga creates the way of the balanced state of mind in all walks of life and gives one efficiency in the execution of one's actions." So, to find peace in the tough parts of being a teenager, I started doing yoga.

Meditation was another spiritual practice my dad loved. Prayer was another. He told me once that meditation could make the world a better place and demanded that I start doing it every day. When asked about that, he would quote Jiddu Krishnamurti and say, "Meditation is not a way to get somewhere." My dad taught me many different ways to meditate, from simple things like focusing on my breath to more advanced techniques like visualising. Anulom Vilom, a type of pranayama that helps balance the body's right and left blood flows, was one of his best exercises. It was he who taught me that the breath is the link between the body and the mind. Through silent meditation, I learned how to clear my mind, focus, and connect with my inner self. It turned into a habit that helped me find peace and order during a time when I was growing up that was sometimes very rough.

We also believed that ceremonies were an important part of faith. My dad thought that ceremonies could help people connect with God if they were done with the right purpose and passion. There was a small prayer meeting in our home every night. We lit a diya and gave flowers to the god of our home. "Let the GOD rest next to me," my dad told me one time. This only means that we should let God into our lives. These ceremonies were not only a way to pray, but also to remember to be grateful and pay attention. Sri Sri Ravi Shankar once said, "Action in hands, quietness in heart." My dad used to have this quote at home. We started having family prayers and discussing happy moments and issues that bothered us. It also provided comfort in prayer during such occasions.

This was the kind of transformation that these spiritual activities brought to our lives. Happiness, my dad once told me, lies in accepting oneself. It is all about the ability to live on one's own according to him; happiness is all about being with people and not possessing many things in life. This philosophy was supported by many other heads of spiritual movements, such as Dalai Lama: "Happiness is not something that is ready-made. It comes from your own actions." Yoga, meditation and rituals contributed to my understanding of how things should be done and become positive and constructive in everyday life approach.

In addition to praying and meditating alone, my dad liked spiritual events that were held in groups. He normally set up family get-togethers where we talked about things like our spirituality, our own lives, and other things. These platforms pushed people to work together and made it clear that anyone can learn from anyone else. "Supporting Not Interfering" was something my dad always said. He meant that if you really want to help someone, you have to let them grow on their own. The talks turned exciting and motivating, and it was interesting to learn how important it is to share a faith experience.

One of the most important pieces of advice my dad ever gave me was to use positive mantras. His belief was that our thoughts make our world and that positive affirmations can change how we feel. He told us to always be positive and learn to love ourselves by saying "I allow, I deserve, I accept." He told me to start using mantras every day, so I did. When said over and over with a lot of confidence, these few words gave me faith and a "can-do" attitude about life.

My dad also talked a lot about how nature plays a part in being magical. So, he came up with the idea that being close to nature is a good way to worship and kill yourself. His quotes from the Bible and the idea that nature was like a screen where one could see their own soul were common. Because of what he taught me, I chose to spend a lot of time outside, maybe walking in the park or just sitting under a tree. These times in nature gave me ideas and peace, and they made me feel more connected to the world around me.

Forgiving and letting go were the other two important parts of our soul search. "The person who serves the best benefits the most," my dad used to say. He meant that holding a grudge or having bad feelings towards someone is bad for your health. Forgiving others and being able to let go of anger and bitterness were big parts of my spiritual healing. It helped me get rid of bad vibes and make room in my life for good things. Buddha said, "Holding on to anger is like drinking poison and expecting the other person to die." This message was backed up by his words. Forging is how I learned that criticism is pointless and how to open my heart to love and kindness.

As a result, the following spirituality through yoga, meditation, and rituals with the help of my father, Vaibhav Gupta, has been very interesting for me. If you want to know how to find true happiness, read his book "Happiness: How, When & Why.'" It's like a lamp that shines a light on the path to faith. Due to these lessons, I know that rituals, yoga, and meditation make my life better and help me find peace and balance within myself. I always try to remember these moral lessons as I continue to learn and grow because I know that they will make me happier in the long run. Thank you to my father and the other spiritual people in our lives, this is a clear sign of how insightful these practices are for me.

Chapter 4

Finding Joy in Simple Pleasures

Celebrating festivals, food, and daily rituals

My father narrated childhood experiences to me, and he was always cheerful every time. It has also changed my outlook on what he used to refer to as happiness of enjoying what life has to offer positively. The subjects of the most interesting events were narrated to me by my dad. The Indians love their holidays, and especially the ones we have here are grand, colourful affairs, and the parties are not any different. My dad once said to me that, I used to be fond of such things when I was a child. "Like everything else, festivals are not about the fizzer and the glare," he would often state. It is all about quality time and moments with loved ones, having fun and sharing the moments – the childhood celebration of Diwali was always a delight for him. He would explain how he and his friends would create patterns or designs on the floor using coloured powders and make lamps to light and burst firecrackers. He once said to me Diwali is not the light outside but the lights within us the lights of happiness and humanity. Lighting of the diya he said overcame the darkness or evil, the significance of lighting the diya as small as it may seem, was important to me and made me happy.

Food was also an important component of these festivities Being a great food lover, my father especially cherished the Indian sweets: 'Fresh sweets would be made on such occasions, the smell of laddoo or jalebi filled the house and to eat sweets made by mothers with love made one happy'. He liked to refer to the adage "good food is the root of true happiness" and how a meal, lovingly prepared and eaten with family and friends can unite people.

Apart from festivals, my father had the simplicity of life and in every small and big occurrence of life, he looked forward to happiness. He had been a troublemaker in his parent's house, in fact, the worst-behaved child when he was growing up, but he valued the things that are taken for granted in childhood such as waking up in the morning and going to school among other activities. He would do this and later sleep early in the evening, arise early in the morning, pray with his family and then have breakfast with them. "Such moments," he could say, "are the true pleasures of life. " The meal time, the funny stories during the breakfast, and the feeling of being with friends all made him happy.

There is one of his stories that I recall to this day and that is the story of how he used to walk to school. Thus, even though my father was naughty, he enjoyed these walks. For them, those were not only ways of getting to school, but an exciting journey in itself. He too would go out with his friends, playing with the small stones they found, climbing trees and at times, swimming in the small pond nearby. 'For example, while going for a walk he would say that it was during such occasions he grasped the importance of companionship and the fun of discovering the world', These are the treasures of life he decided to share with me.

My father always used to explain that happiness lies within, and we should learn to take small pleasures in life. He would say, "Do not rush the moments and feel the moment that you're in." Many spiritual leaders shared this thought. For example, Thich Nhat Hanh stated, "The present moment is filled with joy and happiness. If you are attentive, you will see it." My father exemplified this thought and went through his days practising this notion. Whether it was having a cup of tea in the morning, listening to birds singing, or watching the sunset, these simple pleasures of life made him happy.

Food, festivals and ordinary routines were not mere occasions for my father; they were experiences that brought meaning to his life and connected him to his loved ones. There was a book that he liked to quote, by Sri Sri Ravi Shankar, that read "The joy of life is doing what you love, with the people you love". He always delayed the definition of joy as this one and this was the way he saw happiness.

My father also stressed the importance of thankfulness. He always taught me to appreciate the little things in life. "Gratitude," he would say, "turns what we have into enough." He often shared that when he was a child, he was the naughtiest one in the family. One day, he was out at the playground, when he discovered a small bird with a damaged wing. He brought the bird home, tended to it, and fed the bird until it was strong again. He said that the feeling he got from helping that bird was the most satisfying thing that he had ever done. "That I then and there knew the meaning of happiness, for it is in giving and caring for others."

But, the other aspect of living a joyful life by focusing on little things was that he enjoyed nature. My father used to accompany me for nature walks and explain to me the wonders of this world. He once said to me that 'Nature' is a manifestation of God and how creative the Lord is.' I used to want to take a walk with him and literally explore nature and in each walk he used to quote John Muir "In every walk with nature, one receives far more than he seeks". They taught me how to enjoy a blooming flower and the sound of birds, as well as the sight of a flowing river.

The words of wisdom my father passed to me have been of great help to me. One thing that he has done for me is that he encouraged me to look for happiness in the smallest things in life. It is the little things in life such as eating with my family, having a walk in the park, or taking a break and knowing I have done my best in the day. He used to tell me, "Happiness is not about seeking the next big thing." "It is the celebration of the beauty found within the mundaneness of life."

Hence, the notions about happiness derived from the teachings of my father, are as follows. Those tales and the lessons related to them can teach even a stone that happiness is in the gentle joys of life. Sharing happiness at a festival, having tasty meals, and simple everyday practices are not actions but rather meaningful processes that make life valuable. For this reason, as I move forward in life I take these miracles and hold them close because they help me work towards a happier life.

The importance of gratitude and contentment

My father, Vaibhav Gupta, taught me a lot about living a grateful and happy life through his moving book, "Happiness: How, When and Why."When I think about life as a 17-year-old high school student who grew up in a home where folklore is very important, I always think of something my dad told me. Picking happiness in the little things in life is what the three points are all about.

There is always a race to fit in with the material things of life these days, and my dad's words help me understand that true happiness lies in the everyday and unnoticed. My dad once told me, "They are remembered when they are gone" when he saw people who wrote by themselves. This made me want to spend time by myself and write. This quote reminds me to stop and enjoy the simple things in life that are important, like the sun in the morning, friends who make you laugh, and the peace of the evening.

Because it leads to happiness, being thankful is very important. It tells us to accept the changes in our lives without changing who we are. Some people work hard to make big changes, but they don't see that they already need or want a lot of things. So, learning to be thankful can help you accept things as they are, no matter how bad they are.

My father always likes to remind me of this saying, 'the person who serves best, prospers most.' This makes me understand that bettering the lives of others yields happiness. My dad often tells me this quote. This quote has helped me learn that helping others and making their lives better only leads to good things. Everyone is happier when they do small acts of kindness for each other. All of these things make you feel good: helping a friend with their homework, feeding someone who is hungry, or listening to someone talk about their problems or woes.

My dad will sometimes use stories from his own life to explain these ideas. He talks about his childhood, which shows how much kids used to enjoy even the easiest games and activities. They didn't have any fancy toys or gadgets, but they were friends and knew how to have fun and get into trouble. They spent their afternoons doing a variety of things, such as exploring nature and playing both standard games and games that kids would make up on their own. After reading these, I feel like relationships and events are more important than money and other material things when it comes to being happy. I want to share a story from my dad's book that really inspires me: one time, my dad and his friends set up an unplanned cricket game. They only had a wooden bar and a rubber ball because they didn't have any proper gear or a field. They were having a great time, even though they didn't have any resources. They laughed and rallied for each other. This story is a gem about how to keep good habits and be happy with what you have, even if you want more.

My dad taught me that you should always be aware of what is going on around you and live in the moment. He pushes me to do my best in everything I do by saying, "Learn, Grow, Give, Impact." Consciously paying attention helps me enjoy everything I do, like studying, spending time with my family, having fun, etc. Mindfulness trains me to value easy things like eating a home-cooked meal or going for a walk in the park. Being humble and happy are linked to the idea of being cheap. One of them is something my dad always says: "Work for work, not work for money." If our job makes us happy, then we will be happy with what we do every day. By looking for happiness in the process rather than the results, this point of view helps me have a good mood about what I do.

"Building & Leading Tomorrow Together" is another lesson from my dad's book that helps the community and everyone's well-being. People can make their environment happy and more cohesive if they work together and help each other. For example, my dad always encourages me to do things like volunteer work, community service, and working with other people. Not only are they fun, but they also help people feel like they belong and give their lives value. This quote from my dad's book was one of the most important ones for me:

"Beyond material things, experience & knowledge sharing come on top of the excellent karma." It's not good to get caught up in land and worldly things. To do this, we can both motivate others and help them be happy, while also learning from their experiences. This idea inspires me to do things like learning new things, travelling, and making connections with other people that matter.

Our family has several traditions and practices that help us appreciate simple joys. As an example, we say "grace" before we eat as a custom. Each person in the family can say what they are thankful for, which creates an atmosphere of thanksgiving and happiness. Every time we do this, we remember to be grateful for the food on our table, the people in our lives, and the things we have. It was also taught to us by my dad that art can bring happiness. In this way, art, writing, and gardening are all things that help us express ourselves and be happy. He often says, "Mentoring NOT Monitoring to teach." This means that you should promote innovation and individuality. This way of thinking lets me enjoy some of the good things about expressing myself and the fun that comes with it.

When I think about these lessons, I sometimes look to the famous quotes of other great people to encourage me. My dad often talks about the famous quote by Mahatma Gandhi that goes, "Be the change that you want to see in the world." This helps me understand that my job is to bring about good change with the help of other people. It's a warning that the only way to be truly happy is to be true to yourself and the values you hold dear. Radhakrishnan Pillai said, "Be collective; create wealth for each other." This is another deep quote that speaks to me. This sentence fits with what my dad taught me about society and living a better life. It proves that society will be happier and more prosperous if people help and support each other.

The way my dad stressed being thankful and happy makes me think of Dr. Norman Vincent Peale's words, "My favourite prayer for peace is "God grant me the serenity to accept the things I cannot change, the courage to change the things I can, and the wisdom to know the difference." I'm glad my dad was my role model for the rest of my teen years, especially when it came to how important it is to enjoy the little things in life. I've adopted a culture of gratitude and pay close attention to how a minute can be full of valuable moments. My goal is to find happiness in everyday things. My favourite speech that teaches me these valuable lessons and inspires me to live a happy life is the title of my dad's book, "Happiness: How, When, and Why."

Chapter 5

The Power of Community and Social Bonds

The role of community and social gatherings

I think that my close-knit family and active surroundings have had a big effect on how I think about happiness and how important relationships are. The most important thing my dad, Vaibhav Gupta, told me was to get to know your neighbours well and take part in social events. His book "Happiness: 'How, When, and Why'" is full of deep insights that stress how important it is to have a sense of belonging and a shared past. One of the best pieces of advice my dad ever gave me is to always talk to people. He always uses catchy phrases like "Engage, Retain, Grow," which means that people need to take part in group events, make friends, and keep growing as a society. This is the attitude I've lived by my whole life because it makes everyone happy.

This is a very important thing that social events do for our community: they bring people together. When these kinds of events happen, it's like when the family gets together or a show, and everyone is happy. My dad always said, "The person who serves the best profits the most." That quote has helped me get through these hard times. This one could teach us that making other people happy makes us happy too. Celebrating Puja with my community is one of the most beautiful things that has ever happened to me. Families start getting ready for the holiday weeks or even months ahead of time by decorating their homes, making sweets, and planning cultural events. It means that everyone in the town is involved, and the event gets very busy. My dad often says, "ज़िंदगी को जीना आसान नहीं होता, ज़िंदगी को जीना आसान बनाना पड़ता है।" The phrase "Living life isn't easy, but making life easy is essential." sums up how the community helps make life easier and happier despite all the problems.

These events help us understand what it means to feel joy as a group. Everyone's smile, the jokes, and the sense of community really made me believe in the power of community. My dad always told me that the best way to be happy is to spend time with people you care about, like family. "Value change, not change our values," he would remark. As a society and a people, we should always believe that change is good, but we shouldn't forget how important it is to value our neighbours and society as a whole.

Another thing that my dad stressed about the community was the support system that the community has for its members. "Need can be met, Greed cannot be met," he used to say. After reading this quote, I learnt that everyone can get what they need, but greed and other bad habits can't be fixed in society. To give an example, when something bad happens in our neighbourhood, everyone helps each other out by giving money or mental support. Our happiness is increased because this group work makes us safer as a whole.

My dad also believed in the neighbourhood mentoring system. "Mentoring NOT Monitoring to teach" means that you are not to be too forceful when you help others. This way of doing things helps build a mindset of positivity and productivity where everyone can reach their full potential. In our society, older people are always good examples because it's their job to teach the younger people. Traditions of passing on information and values from one generation to the next make social connections stronger and give people a sense of purpose and unity. Meetings and social events are also good times to learn about other countries. My dad always said, "Learn, Grow, Give, Impact," because he thought that everyone should always be willing to learn something new and make the world a better place. These kinds of meetings make us better and smarter, whether they're stories, cultural events, or just casual chats.

The most moving story my dad ever told me was about an effort to clean up the neighbourhood. A group of young people from our neighbourhood planned the drive, which was meant to clean up a park that looked like it had been forgotten. My dad always told me to "Broaden your Minds and Deepen your Roots" when he wanted me to do something good for the world. Everyone participated in the clean-up drive, and there were people of all ages to ensure that the environment was clean. While beautifying the park and making it useful, there was this feeling of pride and joy that words cannot express. This made me more confident that communities can make good changes and can improve the lives of many people.

My dad also points out in the book that people should be empathetic and care for other people in the community. As often as not, he would read, "Compassionate & Courageous" and emphasise the value of caring for others. This is evident in our community, especially when people contribute their efforts in supporting the less privileged, in fundraising, personal counselling, and assisting each other, especially during hard times. Such actions help to unite people and, most importantly, make our existence more joyful as a whole.

My dad used to always say, "Share the knowledge, gain the

wisdom." It's the same thing as sharing our experiences and learning from others. Some of the common methods of exchanging information present in our community include forums, local clubs, discussion groups, and cultural occasions. These interactions not only contribute to personal development but also to friendship formation and the sense that we are all connected. However, it is important to note that community and social relations are very crucial in our lives. My father also used to say that one must be happy and that true happiness is accompanied by having company and friends. My father states, 'If we want to make a plan to succeed, we need to look after culture first. And that culture begins by giving first, getting later' can be said to champion this philosophy. Caring for our community and cultivating healthy interpersonal bonds enhance the overall environment that people in the community experience.

These lessons come in handy as I journey through adolescence with my father. In his book, "Happiness: How, When and Why," the essay underlines the significance of society and interpersonal relationships in the process of living. His knowledge and our family and community experiences have taught me that true pleasure is a shared experience. It can be seen that the self and future generations can be made happier and more peaceful by including the concept of community and social relations.

Lessons learned from communal harmony and support

From when I was a kid, I remember my dad talking about what makes people happy and how being happy is linked to community support and unity. This is a great book full of deep truths and wise words that really helped me when I was trying to figure out what happiness and relationships are all about. In light of these lessons, some of the things he taught me about the community and how important it is for everyone to get along are listed below.

Communal harmony means that people from different backgrounds, cultures, and groups can live and work together without any problems. You have to accept and love the fact that we are all linked and, by extension, all belong. "Happiness comes more easily when we feel good about ourselves without feeling the need for anyone else's approval," my father writes in his book. Self-acceptance is a key part of getting along with people from other communities. People can hear the same words from us when we are at peace with ourselves. It is important for social harmony to grow and stay strong that agnah is present. Being there for each other through good times and bad, and working together to reach common goals is what it's all about. "Happiness lies in the present," my dad used to say, so be there for each other. It makes a difference in someone's life whether you're there for them with words, deeds, or just being there. Building a safe society starts with building trust and relationships with other people.

One of the main ideas my dad wrote about in his book was empathy and understanding. "Happiness is a process and cannot be achieved by simply trying it," My father states. So, part of the process is knowing other people's pain and suffering. So, empathy gives us the power to help and build groups that work well together. My dad liked to tell me stories about how doing good things, like helping a neighbour or giving, made him happy as well. My dad's book is full of positive statements that can inspire people to stick together and be brothers. Dad said "The mind has a tendency to doubt the positive things in life. Doubt the negative and put your trust in the positive." This quote links the idea of positive thought to the idea of community. When we choose to see the good in ourselves and the people around us, we help everyone and encourage them to keep going with their plans.

Society needs to be able to communicate well in order to stay balanced. "Our minds never stop functioning," my father often stated. Only the conscious portion of our minds is accessible to us while we are awake, but our minds are never truly shut off. We need to be able to communicate clearly and with empathy all the time because our minds are always working. It could lead to arguments, but good communication and direct discussion can solve problems and make relationships better. Because of this, religious events play a big part in bringing people together in the community. In his book, my dad talks about different kinds of breathing and meditation that can help people get along and bring society together. His voice explained, "Meditation is considered to be the seventh arm of the eight-fold path of yoga. Meditation may be an ancient ritual, but it is practised to establish a sense of relaxation and inner harmony in cultures all over the world." These habits help people find balance in their relationships, which can be applied to society as a whole.

My father taught me important lessons about coming together to help each other through pain and sorrow. "Suffering is an option; it always has been. We need not suffer every time we face a situation that does not favour us." This idea makes people strong and helps them stick together when things get tough. I think that by doing something like this, one can help someone deal with their problems and live a happy life. Appreciation is another important thing that can help keep the peace in a community setting. My dad writes in his book, "Self-compassion allows us to manage the discomfort of these complaints, and instead turn to the amazing things for which we should be thankful, increasing our satisfaction with life all around us." Being thankful makes us value the help that is easy to find in our neighbourhoods and encourages us to help others who are in need. In his book, my dad also talks about a lot of people who are role models because they show support and understanding for others. The lessons of His Holiness Sri Sri Ravi Shankar, who was his spiritual master and guru, have inspired many people to live a good life. The way my dad loved his parents, siblings, and friends also says a lot about the importance of unity and community.

Thus, my father's lessons were an important source that shaped my views on the importance of supporting and preserving the balance in our community. His comments have helped me learn that how we give back to our communities has a lot to do with how happy we are. Kindness, positive self-talk, helpful conversation, prayer, persistence, gratitude, and being a good example for the community. My father said, "Happiness is living in the moment with joy, awareness and compassion; being free from within, feeling at home with everyone without barriers."

Finally, the lessons of community support and peace are very important to learn. It teaches us that happiness isn't something that only happens to one person but to many people. My dad always says "The day my Thoughts, Words & Actions (मनसा, वाचा, कर्मणा) inspire others to: Dream more, Learn more, Do more, Become More & Grow more, I will consider myself as a Leader." These words have inspired me to work in my neighbourhood and make other people happy.

Chapter 6

Overcoming Adversity with Resilience

Stories of resilience from the author's family and Indian history

Courage is the strength upon which the soul is built, and that can only come from its hardships and continuance. In my childhood, my father taught me persistence through words and actions. His book, "Happiness: 'How, When and Why," is full of good advice on which approach underlines that only perseverance is a key to happiness. "Compassionate & Courageous" was something he said a lot because he wanted me to know that courage always comes with kindness. So many stories of how people have survived have been told to us all through the years. That's why the story of my grandfather, who went through a lot of hard times as a child, is one of the most important. Even though he had trouble with money and couldn't afford to study, he was able to finish school and get a good job. He showed us that we should always try to get through hard times. Being a wise man, my father often says things like Lao Tzu said, "Need can be met, greed cannot be met."

My grandfather's story helps me remind myself that if someone is strong, he can endure anything as things cannot get any worse even if they seem so difficult. "अगर आप किसी की मदद करने में सक्षम हैं, और आप ने किसी की मदद नहीं की, तो समझें आप ने जीवन में कुछ नहीं किया" it means 'if you have the ability to help someone and you did not help that person, then you have done nothing in life. The last part of this sentence was a revelation: resiliency is not only about doing well for yourself but also about helping others when they are in a weak state.' There are many histories of India that reveal how strong people can be, and many generations have been following them. One such story is that of Rani Lakshmibai of Jhansi who fought the British without any regard during the first war of Indian independence in 1857. A lot of courage and motivation were depicted in front of enormous challenges, and she turned out to be a symbol of resistance. My dad used to narrate her story as an example of the need to do the right thing in a society that does not support such a stand. He was very clear about it and said, "Value change, not change our value." He emphasised how crucial it is to be flexible while maintaining such values as truth and perseverance.

The other story from the history of India is the struggle of Mahatma Gandhi, who fought against the British colonisation of India, and his fight lacked endurance. His famous quote 'Be the change that you want to see in this world' is a reminder that resilience is about changing the world, starting with oneself with perseverance and determination. My father used the example of Gandhiji's life and his messages to me to persevere in the face of hardship and to work towards a change in society without violence.

For instance, in my family, my dad has always been an inspiring figure. At a certain point in our lives, the family struggled with finances, yet he did not lose faith. "Work for work, not work for money," he would always tell us. This meant that the effort that goes into work was more important than the money that comes at the end. Our family was able to get through the hardest times and come out stronger because he was determined and thought positively. "Thoroughly used up self before I leave" is a favourite quote of my dad's that he always told me and my brothers. In simple terms, this means that people should do their best work before time runs out. My life has always been guided by the idea that we should always do our best, no matter what. That helped me learn that being resilient means pushing ourselves to be the best we can be, even when things are hard.

Being resilient also means having help from family and friends. There is no doubt that family is best when things are hard, and everyone is there to help each other. My dad always said, "Family values, principles, and goals," to stress that the values and principles of our family are what make us strong. These are some of the ideals that have kept our family strong and united no matter what. In addition to stories about people and families, my dad also found inspiration in spiritual beliefs. He often said, "Sewa- मनसा, वाचा, कर्मणा" which means to serve with our mind, our words, and our deeds. The above saying talks about how important it is to be humble and determined when helping other people. I learnt that real power isn't just about how strong someone is but how they can help others and improve their lives.

This is also related to resilience, which is how we learn from the things that go wrong and the hard things that happen in our lives. Every time I fail, my dad would tell me, it's a chance to learn and become a better person. "Learn, Grow, Give, Impact" was something he used to say. It means that every mistake is a chance to learn, grow, and make a difference in other people's lives. For me, this has helped me develop a strong and positive attitude when facing difficulties. There is one quote that sums up the most important thing my dad taught me: "What makes us very special? Our ability to share what we know, irrespective of our level of achievements." This quote shows that one of the best things about us is that we can teach others, no matter how much we have already done in our own lives. People will be able to learn from their mistakes and be inspired to get through their problems.

Life has changed a lot for me because of the morals my family taught me and the history of India. In reading about great people and listening to my dad, I learnt that the only way to be happy in life is to keep going. Even now that I'm a teenager, these lessons are still useful to me because they teach me that no matter what, I can always pick myself up and have a good attitude about life. Values, family, and community give people the resilience and strength to face life's challenges with courage and compassion, which leads to a better and more satisfying life.

Strategies for developing mental strength and perseverance

Suffering is a reality of life, and building resilience and endurance is something that people should strive for. As a 17-year-old motivated by my father, I have come to understand that the definition of resilience is not just about suffering but coming out on the other end as a better person. He often remarked, "The mind has a tendency to doubt the positive things in life. Doubt the negative and put your trust in the positive." This is one of the most important aspects of developing a strong and effective coping mechanism. His book, "Happiness: "How, When and Why," is replete with advice and guidance on how to build and nurture mental toughness. The first pillar of mental strength is cultivating a positive attitude. My father used to tell me that there is always a silver lining in every cloud. He would tell me things like, 'Don't ever think my way is a highway' or 'Don't ever think my way or no way,' which taught me the importance of being able to adapt and be ready to change as a form of strength. This approach has helped me to change my perception of the difficulties that are present in life as being positive rather than negative.

Planners that include both mental and physical tasks are another useful strategy. This saying, "T. I. M. E." (Thankfulness, Insight, Meditation, Exercise) by Jay Shetty, impressed my dad a lot. Thoughts are kept busy, and mental strength is built through yoga and meditation. These habits have become normal for me because they help me stay calm and focused even when things are crazy. Having goals that one can reach and working hard to reach them is another way to improve their mental strength. "Engage, Retain, Grow" were the words my dad always taught me. I knew he meant I should never lose focus and always do my best. These statements are true because setting realistic goals and recognising our progress helps us build confidence and persistence. With this plan, I've made sure I don't give up when things get tough and that I stay inspired.

Another way of building power is through assembling a powerful network. My dad's book also tells me that when people join hands, they are more powerful. He once said, "Happiness comes more easily when we feel good about ourselves without feeling the need for anyone else's approval. " This trust in oneself comes from having a good network. He would say, "Learn, Grow, Give, Impact," to encourage me to seek advice from others and then offer advice to others. Being surrounded by good people is always helpful in lifting our morale and guiding us on the right thing to do in the event of a challenge. Another thing that can help make one stronger mentally is to give thanks. I believe that when my dad said to us, 'The person who serves the best, profits the most', this helped us learn about being grateful. This is good because it means that we can easily let go of the negative aspects of life by just concentrating on the positive side of life and being grateful for it. It has assisted me to have a good attitude about life, though there have been many problems, it has kept me focused.

Dealing with loss and setbacks is another part of becoming more resilient. "Failures are the stepping stones to success," my dad would tell me when I needed to cheer myself up. By thinking about our mistakes and failures, we can make our minds stronger and more resilient. I have also been able to keep a positive outlook on work by seeing problems as challenges I need to beat. Self-compassion is another thing that makes us resilient. With this method, I've been able to build emotional capital and stay focused when things get tough.

One of the other important lessons my dad taught me was the importance of balance in life. He always said, "Work for work, not money." This meant that people should love what they do and not expect to be paid for it. This means that doing things that make one happy and content helps one to become more mentally tough and positive. It taught me how to balance work and home life and how important it is to look after myself. Doing artistic things is another way to make our minds stronger. "ज्ञान, योग, धारणा, सेवा" meant to know things, do yoga, meditate, and help other people. Painting, writing, or playing an instrument are all things that can help a person deal with stress and get stronger. There is a strong link between being mentally and physically healthy. Also, I think it's important to add that my dad's book has good ideas for living a healthy life. "A peaceful mind has the power to reach out to God and make some kind of connection with him," he said many times. "We all know that to reach out to God would mean happiness in some way." The mind and body both need to exercise, eat right, and get enough sleep. Being physically healthy is important for our mental health because it helps us deal with worry and other problems. Doing these things has brought me joy and helped me relax when things were hard in my life.

The thought of resilience is also helped by having a purpose in life. My dad used to tell me, "Purpose to live for something more than yourself." That helped me understand that there are many reasons to live and fight for something, even when things aren't going well. This means that we can set goals that make sense and work towards them, which is good for our mental health and helps us keep our eyes on the prize. Taking this method has helped me stay focused on my goals and determined, especially when things get tough. So, the keys to success and happiness in life are building character, being mentally tough, and sticking with things even when they get hard. From my dad and my own life, I've learnt that being resilient means having a positive outlook on life, setting goals that one can reach, surrounding oneself with supportive people, and being grateful. for what one does have, learning from one's errors, being kind to oneself, living a healthy life, being creative, finding meaning in life, and helping others. All of these tactics have helped me become mentally tough so that I can handle any tough situation in life. By following these rules, a person can deal with problems and create a happy, purposeful life.

Chapter 7

Education and Personal Growth

The importance of education

One of the most important things for human growth has always been education. My family is from India, and my dad, Vaibhav Gupta, always puts a lot of value on learning. The lessons my dad taught me, summed up in his book "Happiness: How, When, and Why?" have shaped how I think about school. The expression "People who write by themselves are remembered when they are gone" was one that he would frequently recite. He was referring to the notion that knowledge is significant and that people's accomplishments are significant and long-lasting.

I've known since I was a child that education wasn't just a way to get to work after finishing school. As my dad always said, "Happiness is a process and cannot be achieved by simply trying it." This sentence is wise when it comes to the process of getting educated. Gurudev Sri Sri Ravi Shankar said, "Happiness is living in the moment with joy, awareness, and compassion; being free from within, feeling at home with everyone without barriers." This quote describes the process of learning, which is the process of opening the mind to new ideas. This is where the seeds of growth and happiness lie. Being educated in this way is like discovering something new every day; each lesson brings you closer to knowing yourself and the world around you.

In our family, education was never seen as a way to get a job.

Instead, it was seen as a way to become a good person. My dad once told me, "Our minds never stop functioning. We can access only the conscious part of our minds when we are awake, but our minds never stop." We can only use the aware part of our minds when we're awake. But our minds never stop. The conscious mind is active when a person is awake, but the mind never sleeps. This is where schooling comes in handy. Our mind grows in terms of what we know and how we feel because it supports our need to learn and use our interests. This focus on emotional intelligence has taught me more about how to communicate honestly, solve problems, and negotiate in both my personal and professional life. By learning these skills, I've improved my relationships with other people and my ability to get along with others in general. I've also learnt how to handle different social situations.

My dad always told me that education is something that can be done throughout one's life. "पढ़े लिखे होने से अच्छा है, पढ़ते लिखते रहना," which means "It is better to keep reading and learning than just being educated." This quote has always meant a lot to me because it reminds me that learning doesn't just happen in the classroom. It's something that happens all the time, not just in school. It happens even after you finish learning. Because of my father's view on lifelong learning, I will always be interested and willing to learn new things. When I was a kid, the most important thing my dad ever told me was that knowledge makes you strong. He would say over and over, "ज्ञान, योग, धारणा, सेवा" which means "knowledge, yoga, control, and service." This unique way of teaching has shown me that learning is more than just getting more information. It's also about growing in body, mind, and spirit. Including all of these things in my life has given me a more balanced view, which has helped me get through many difficult situations.

Learning was a particularly important topic that was emphasised in my father's lessons, and the importance of this was emphasised to a great extent by his ideals of discipline and laboriousness. He always told me things like, "Don't ever think my way is a highway" or "Don't ever think my way or no way" to teach me that the way to success isn't always clear and that it's good to be flexible. It has helped me stay on track with my goals, even when things get tough, and it has given me a general idea that hard work and determination pay off in both school and personal life. In addition to teaching me self-discipline, my dad also pushed me to be humble and thankful so that I could go to school. "The person who serves the best, profits the most" was a quote he always used to show that it's good to help other people. During my time at school, I have maintained this concept in my interactions with teachers and peers, focussing on being thankful for the chances I have been given and eager to help others learn. By being humble and willing to help others, I've become able to appreciate the work that others do and accept that learning is a group activity.

The relevance of education in the development of societal obligations and patriotism was something that my father emphasised in addition to the necessity of individual progress. He was heard to say, "If we want to make a plan to succeed, we need to look after culture first And that culture begins by giving first, getting later." This quote made me think about how important it is for my education to have a good effect on the world. Being an involved member of the fight for justice and equality, volunteering, and social causes has taught me that education is a tool that can be used to help other people live better lives.

It's also important to remember that education plays a big part in developing "emotional" resilience. Getting educated is the best way to deal with tough times because it helps you understand and think things through. "Suffering is an option; it always has been," says my dad in his book. "We don't have to suffer every time something goes wrong for us." It's not necessary for us to suffer every time something goes wrong. We can handle the problems that come up in life better if we have a good education. It has also helped me deal with the problems that come with being a teenager and figure out who I am. Putting what my dad taught me into practice every day has helped me develop core values like honesty, persistence, and the importance of activities that have meaning for me. These values will help me in all the things I do.

Without a doubt, education is a helpful tool that can help a person become a better person. Through watching my dad and going through my own life, I've learnt that education isn't just about facts; it's also about the whole person, inside and out. Learning how to be self-controlled, persistent, humble, thankful, aware of oneself and others, empathetic, and fair is a strong way to improve oneself and become the best one can be. My dad always told me to "Learn, Grow, Give, Impact." This phrase has always made me realise that education is not a straight line, but a circle.

Continuous learning and self-improvement are keys to happiness

It shows how important it is to keep learning and growing as a person because those are the things that make people happy. My father always brought up the importance of learning and how it could help with personal growth and education. I liked the program's ideas and understood the value of education and the life-changing effects that come with reading his book "Happiness: How, When, and Why." He used the term "Learn, Grow, Give, Impact" a lot. These are words I try to live by every day. A big part of my dad's book is also about the idea of happiness as a process, not a state. "Happiness comes more easily when we feel good about ourselves without feeling the need for anyone else's approval," he said. In other words, we're usually happy when we're okay with who we are and don't need other people to validate our feelings. This peace and joy come from being proud of yourself, which comes from wanting to learn and grow as a person. One of the most important things my dad told me is how important it is to get a good education. "The mind has a tendency to doubt positive things in life. It is natural to doubt negatives and believe in positives." he would tell me over and over again. It's normal to doubt bad things and trust good things. This quote has become my personal motto whenever I want to learn something new. Having a positive outlook can really help one stay motivated to learn because it helps one understand that the goal is not to avoid losing, but to increase the likelihood of succeeding by learning and using what's been learnt.

My dad used to think about academic achievement in a very broad way. He says that education is more than just books and chalkboards. Ideas, connections, and everything else you learn in everyday life are all part of it. As he put it, "Meditation is considered to be the seventh arm of the eight-fold path of yoga. Meditation may be an ancient ritual, but it is practised to establish a sense of relaxation and inner harmony in cultures all over the world." Even though meditation is an old practice, people from all over the world do it to calm down and find inner peace. Of course, this is the basis for both mental and emotional health and well-being. The idea of learning new things throughout every day is becoming even more important in today's world where information is always growing. This is because technology changes quickly and the global economy is always changing, so people need to keep their knowledge and skills up to date. My dad says that there's nothing wrong with being ready for lessons whenever they come up. "Desires and wishes are different. Though they might be quite similar, they are never the same." he used to say. They are never the same, even if they look a lot alike. These words assist in expounding the notion that it is essential that people continuously learn new things all the time. The desire to be and become better people can be a greater want that makes one happy even if the want is fleeting.

Once my dad informed me that it is also possible to progress in life by setting and achieving goals. He indeed stated, "We must accept the presence of pain and how it makes us feel instead of being in disapproval of it, its presence is real, and we must face it." Indeed, it is really there, and cannot be thrown away. This indicates that acceptance is one of the most crucial things to do in order to improve oneself. This is the reason why people should set goals that are realistic and appreciate the process of self-improvement as well as any achievements, even the slightest ones. It gives people confidence and satisfaction, making them happy when they put their best in anything they do. It's also part of continuing to learn to get rid of old ways of thinking and acting. According to my dad's book, we have to give up some things in order to move forward. "To truly learn something, we have to unlearn it first," he said. I will never forget this idea because it taught me how important it is to stay fresh and open to new ideas. People often learn something, but then forget it. Then they need to be taught the same thing again after a while. Having this experience is important for the learners' growth because it helps them learn how to handle change in their lives.

As part of learning and improving myself, my dad also showed me how to share information with others and help them grow. In addition to growing as a person, he thought that real happiness comes from seeing other people grow. He told them that the only way to find real happiness is to live in the present:" "Happiness lies in the present,". This idea definitely helps people understand why it's important to teach and be there for them. Every single thing I've read in my dad's book has changed how I think about learning and growing as a person. Education isn't a long way to get to a certain point; it's a trip that lasts a lifetime and is marked by growth, vigour, and personal change. We can definitely do this by always learning new things, setting realistic goals, letting go of old ideas, and sharing what we know with others. My dad said, "Happiness is living in the moment with joy, awareness, and compassion; being free from within and feeling at home with everyone without barriers,". People should keep these lessons in mind and understand that the only way to be healthy and happy is to learn and grow as people.

Chapter 8

Balancing Tradition and Modernity

Navigating the challenges of modern life while honouring traditions

Traditional issues and concerns about progress have become more important when a tradition needs to adapt to changes in technology and a society that is becoming more globalised. I understand that balancing life is possible and important because of these lessons from my dad's book. My dad gives us good advice on how to do well in today's world while keeping true to ourselves by using his own life experiences and examples from well-known scholars. This chapter will use examples from his lessons to talk about progress and tradition. Many Indian families struggle to find the right balance between taking advantage of new possibilities and staying true to their traditions. As a child, my dad would talk to us about how to keep our culture alive while also accepting that things will change. His lessons, which are summed up in his book "Happiness: How, When, and Why," have changed the way I think about this balance the most.

Culture is how we relate to each other and to the world around us. It's like a foundation that helps us know who we are. As a way to set rules for society, wisdom is the practice of things that have been passed down from one generation to the next. With all of its possibilities and challenges, modern life often requires people to get past problems and adapt to new situations. But this kind of adapting doesn't mean giving up on culture or custom. My dad always said, "Happiness comes more easily when we feel good about ourselves without feeling the need for anyone else's approval." That's why it's important to accept yourself based on your society when dealing with problems in the present. People today have a hard time with this because they try to stick to rules and routines. People in the modern world are forced to focus on getting rich at the expense of their racial identity, which makes them feel like they are missing something cultural. My dad liked to quote Gurudev Sri Sri Ravi Shankar. He once said, "Purity in heart, clarity in mind, sincerity in action, and contentment is the formula for happiness." These words make me think that maybe what makes someone happy is not the outcome, but the honesty with which they act.

In our rush to get better, we often forget about the culture that makes us who we are. But my dad always told me that tradition and technology don't have to be at odds with each other. They can live together in peace. He said in his writing, "Happiness is a process and cannot be achieved by simply trying it. " Finding happiness means finding a way to balance the needs of today's society with its values, while still respecting both. It is possible to accept change and try new things in my work while still honouring the traditions of my people, that's what I've learnt. The reason for this is that the clash of old and new ideas can be very painful when trying to combine the traditional and the modern. For example, conservatism can stress the importance of community and family duties, while modernism can stress the importance of individualism and taking care of oneself. This didn't bother my dad because he made sure I knew how important it was to have friends and be involved in society. He was always saying "family values, principles, and goals," the explanation being love, respect, and support for each other no matter what happens in the house or outside.

Another problem is that technology is always changing and moving forward very quickly. Tech makes our lives easier, but it also pulls us farther away from our roots and the people we care about. My father was always informed about both the old and new generation and he used to advise me to be wise when using technology. He used to say, "Balance is the key to a happy life," which means that technology should never be our boss and should always be used to help us. This point of view has helped me make the most of modern technology while still honouring my cultural ideals. I learnt from my dad how important it is to be connected to your roots through traditional festivals and rituals in the past. He wants to talk about crazy things that happened when our family celebrated holidays like Diwali, Holi, and Raksha Bandhan with a lot of fun and happiness. It is important to remember that these celebrations were not just about following customs; they were also about getting to know each other, having fun, and being a part of the community. Following language, my dad stressed how important it is to pay attention to our older people. Roosevelt once said, "Happiness is not a goal; it's a by-product of a life well-lived." He often used those words. In fact, adults know this because they have been through all the stages of life. People who listen to their stories may learn useful things about how to live in the modern world while still following traditional ideals.

My dad used to tell me, ' परिश्रम में नहीं है परमात्मा, विश्राम में है राम, 'which means that we can be happy in our daily lives as well as in faith. He insisted that we could have both our worldly jobs and our traditional morals and still have a better life. This knowledge has helped me find a balance between my traditional beliefs and the needs of the modern world. Most of the time, people today forget what's important and only care about getting ahead and making money. On the other hand, my dad taught me that you should follow your dreams without forgetting your traditions. "What we possess is temporary; what we become is permanent," was one of his many sermons about how greedy people are and how important character is forever. Using what I learnt from my dad has helped me live a healthy life in the modern world while still honouring my culture. The things he taught me have helped me respect our cultures and given me the tools I need to deal with a world that is always changing. Being able to live a fuller and more satisfying life based on personal values while also being open to change is a good thing about this balance.

A balance between progress and cultural roots

It's hard for Indian families to find a balance between modernisation and traditional traditions, and my family was no different. I remember when I was a kid, my dad would tell me what this balance meant. Happiness: How, When, and Why, his book, has been a lighthouse for me, showing me how to make the most of both worlds. This tells us about tradition, which means the ideals and habits that have been passed down from generation to generation. My dad always stressed how important these customs were."सदाचार और सच्चाई ही जीवन का असली आधार है," "And more on morals and honesty are the only virtues that make life worth living," he used to say. These techniques are not out of date; they are still useful ways to live in peace and happiness in the modern world.

But my dad also taught me to be open to the changes that the modern world brings. He knew that customs were important, but they shouldn't stop people from making changes. Radhakrishnan Pillai once said, "Be collective, create wealth for each other," He often repeated this. This way of thinking helped me understand how important change and growth are, especially for social and personal growth. People have a hard time when they have to adopt new ideas and innovations while also staying important to their culture. One important social setting where we experience this balance is in the way we connect with each other and do things in our daily lives. For instance, while our family loves the customs of eating together and talking about our lives, we also know how useful it is to use different gadgets in our daily lives. "Adapt to change but don't change your core values." he used to tell me. It helps me understand that while working, one can switch to new technologies and processes as long as they don't change who the entity is.

A second place where tradition and technology mix is in festivals and rituals. My dad told me that they used to celebrate holidays with a lot of joy and strict rules. He would talk to me about Diwali, Holi, and Raksha Bandhan and how they bring people together and make them happy. It was Kumar Vishwas who said, "ताकत पूजनीय नहीं होती, प्रभाव पूजनीय होता है" which means that people worship control rather than power. This taught me that the real value of these events is not the things they give you, but the memories and bonds they make. Besides being flexible, my dad stressed how important it is to keep learning throughout your life. Being educated is something that can connect the old and the new for him. Dad also said, "Continuous learning and self-improvement are keys to happiness." As learners, we will always know about new things that are happening in the world and be up-to-date on them. We will also have the understanding of traditional knowledge to help us make decisions.

Mindfulness is a technique that can help people in both modern times and traditional times, and my dad really liked it. He said, "Mindfulness helps us stay present, reducing anxiety about the future and regrets about the past, thereby enhancing our resilience." In terms of both custom and modernity, mindfulness helps us live in the present while still keeping the culture alive. It helps us deal with the difficulties of modern life with a calm mind and keeps us from losing touch with our roots. As well, my dad talked about how the community can keep the best parts of both old and new things alive. "Support from family and friends is vital for resilience." he wrote. In fact, family and friends should be the most important things to people in the modern world. People feel like they are part of a group and have the security that comes from tradition as they work towards modern goals. He often quoted Mahatma Gandhi, "Be the change you want to see in the world." This showed how important it was to be real while also being open to new ideas and experiences. This has helped me understand how important schoolwork is and how important it is to learn from our parents and other older people.

People often forget about the important things they want to achieve in their lives in this high-tech world. But one day my dad said to me that the secret of being a happy and satisfied person is a healthy life. He ever said, "What we possess is temporary; what we become is permanent." This made me embrace a lifestyle of character over substance. My dad taught me one of the most valuable lessons in life: it is essential to care about people and the community. Once he used to say, "The person who serves the best, profits the most." This helped me understand that it is my responsibility to work for the welfare of my neighbours. Living in a broken culture, it is very crucial for individuals to remain connected and be concerned about each other's welfare. With regard to this part of custom and modernity, there are also decisions that have to be made concerning how one is to live and what one is to do. For example, we like to use and appreciate new technologies and goods, and we attempt to be environmentally friendly. My dad used to tell me, "If we want to make a plan to succeed, we need to look after culture first. And that culture begins by giving first, getting later." It's not easy to find a balance between the two, but the trip is worth it. He told me how to go about this, and I've learnt to accept both the old and the new ways of doing things in society. He would say things like, "Knowledge, yoga, meditation, service." He would then say that these things are timeless and can help us deal with the problems of today.

Overall, my dad's good advice taught me that you don't have to give up modern technology to embrace your ethnic customs. In this way, we can find a work-life balance that makes our lives better and lets us stay connected to our past while looking to the future. He helped me see that balance is beautiful and important in every part of our lives and in the world around us. To back up both tradition and the desire for change, my dad quoted Malala Yousafzai and said, "Change requires courage, hope, and ambition." As a result of this balance, I came up with the plans and guidelines I will follow to keep the things that set us apart from current trends while also keeping what makes us unique as a family and as individuals.

Chapter 9

The Role of Festivals and Celebrations

How festivals contribute to communal joy and personal happiness

I grew up in an Indian family, so there was always a lot of Indian culture at home. My dad's book, "Happiness: How, When, and Why," made me understand the importance of holidays and celebrations in our lives much better. Of course, holidays are celebrations of culture and traditions. But they're also celebrations of coming together and making beautiful memories. In a social setting, they are most useful for making more people happy, both in groups and on their own. Every holiday was enjoyed in style, and I mean lots of style, our home. It was true during those festivals that my father used to say the proverb, 'Happiness multiplies when shared'. It also made sure that everyone got together to celebrate by making it so that family distance and time didn't matter. These times brought our family as much happiness and getting to spend time together as anyone could want. Holidays like Diwali, Holi, Navratri, and Janmashtami were always looked forward to for the traditions and just to spend time with family and friends.

There was also Navratri in our home, which is nine nights of dancing and prayer. My dad always said that Navratri wasn't just a time to pray and fast; it was also a time to honour women and Shakti. As he often said, "Empowerment begins at home." During Navratri, we would enjoy how women in the family were getting stronger. Garba and Dandiya are dance styles that bring people together. Dancing under the stars makes everyone happy. On Krishna Janmashtami, the day Lord Krishna was born, there was a lot of love and happiness. My dad used to tell me stories about Krishna. He said that Krishna was both naughty and smart and that Krishna would teach and play at the same time. Happiness comes from giving. "Life is about finding joy in simple pleasures and deep wisdom in everyday moments, " he said. Maybe that's a good way to sum up what life is all about. The moving songs, acting out Krishna's childhood, and the celebration of his birth at midnight made everyone feel religious and joyful. Through Janmashtami, all I learnt was that spirituality and enjoyment go together, and that's where life's core is.

Ganesh Chaturthi, the festival for Lord Ganesha, was another great event. With more thought, the placement of Ganesha statues, the daily prayers, and the soaking all showed unity and religiousness. It's something my dad always says: "The person who serves the best profits the most." It helps us remember to be helpful. During Ganesh Chaturthi, we would help out with community welfare, which meant that we were part of making sure the events went smoothly. During this event, I first learnt how important volunteering is and how good it feels to help other people. People used to celebrate Makar Sankranti by eating food from the earth. It was also a harvest time. I remembered that this holiday, which is about the Sun moving into the Capricorn sign, was taught to me by my father. He also shared posts like "Gratitude is the foundation of happiness." He told everyone, young and old, to be thankful for the food they ate and the crops they grew. On this particular day, kite flying was part of the practice, which was something that everyone was looking forward to. In the past, during Makar Sankranti, one of India's oldest harvest festivals, people ate things that grew in the ground. It was also time to harvest, pay bills, and get back to our normal daily tasks and habits. As I read this one about the Sun entering the sign of Capricorn, I remembered something my dad taught me. On his blog, he also wrote things like "Gratitude is the foundation of happiness." His words inspired people of all ages and told them to be thankful for the crops they grew and the food they ate. One thing we liked about this practice was flying kites on this day. Some people have gone to the area to unwind, work out in nature, enjoy the winter sun, or spend time with family and friends. Makar Sankranti taught us to be happy and grateful for the things we have in our lives and to accept the gifts that come from nature.

They taught me to be grateful for what I have and to take what life gives me."Gratitude is the foundation of happiness. Diwali is a reminder that even in the darkest times, light will always prevail". People all over the world celebrate Diwali, an important Indian holiday that has a message: no matter how strong the darkness is, light will always win. It was filmed during the holiday of Diwali, when divine light drives out darkness and brings wealth and luck. In honour of the holiday, I cleaned my house, made a rangoli in front of it, and gave candy to my friends and neighbours. We felt like we needed to clean up, share, and enjoy the holiday mood. It was clear from the diyas that good had won over evil, that stupidity had been wiped out, and that hope had come from despair. Lamps called Diyas were used to show that light will triumph over darkness or that smarts will beat stupidity.

A well-known example of this is Holi, the holiday of colours. I heard from my dad that the event showed how beautiful life is. He would say, "Holi is a reminder that life, like colours, is meant to be lived in all its hues." Splashing colours at each other was a fun game, but it was also a sign of letting go of any anger going on. For me, Holi was a holiday to relax and enjoy every moment. It was a break from everyday life. Holi, the holiday of colours, was another family favourite. My dad would talk about how he and his friends used to celebrate Holi as kids by throwing paints and water at each other and making a mess of bright colours. People used to hear him say, "खुले रहो, खिले रहो और खेलते रहो, जीवन एक खेल है," which means "be open, be happy, and keep playing; life is a game." He used to tell people to be open, happy, and fun in their daily lives. The festival of colours Holi taught me how important it is to forgive others and greet everyone with a smile. That was a time to fix broken fences, start over, and welcome life. Also, I felt like I belonged because all of my friends and neighbours enjoyed the festival. Getting ready for events was just as much fun as going to them. Besides that, the planning, the hopes, and the work that went into making sure each event was unique added to the happiness. My dad always said that the way you do something is just as important as the end result. "Thoroughly used up self before I leave," he would tell them, telling them to work as hard as they could on a job. This way of thinking could be seen in how the holidays were organised and planned. Every detail was carefully thought out, from making traditional treats like sweets and savoury foods to setting up decorations and family activities. Talking about the lovely things, there is nothing better than people being happy together, especially during the festivals. It gives a chance for people to unite and meet regardless of the social, economical, and cultural differences. This was evident during festivals when the spirit of giving and sharing was at its best. Whether the occasion included giving out sweets, contributing in one way or another to the needy, or having a meal with the neighbours, festivals created togetherness and joy.

Celebrations of festivals were also a way to remember the customs and values of a society. They helped one group share its knowledge and ways of life with another. The family was not the only group that celebrated at festivals; the whole neighbourhood also took part. We learnt about other holidays besides Eid while having fun with our Muslim friends. My dad told us to go to Eid events because they would teach us about how different religions work. He would say over and over, "Diversity is our strength," pushing for unity and understanding between the different Indian groups. With all of its delicious sweets and meals, Eid really was a great example of how to share and respect other cultures. I learnt from Eid that it's okay for people to be different and that those differences should be valued and accepted. My dad thought that community and ties with other people were important parts of life. He would tell everyone, "Be collective, create wealth for each other," to remind them how important it was to work together. I remember my dad telling me that Eid is also a holiday for forgiving each other and making peace. Rumi, the great thinker, once said, "The wound is the place where the Light enters you." He would also say this. In the spirit of Eid, my dad told us, we should forgive those who hurt us and show love from the bottom of our hearts. This lesson about forgiving is still very important to me. It makes me think that hanging on to anger and resentment and not showing love to others is not the way to true happiness. The happy mood that Christmas brought into our home made my dad happy. "I will honour Christmas in my heart and try to keep it all the year" by Charles Dickens was something he often said. For my dad, Christmas wasn't about the holiday itself, but about the ideals that went along with it, like love, charity, and kindness. It was his way of telling me that we should keep the spirit of Christmas alive all year by being kind to other people.

Families were more united during festivals because they made everyone respect each other and feel like they were part of the same group. It was a time to accept each other as people and as individuals who make up one culture or the other.

Because of this, celebrations and holidays are very important for making people and groups happy. It brings people together, makes them feel like they belong, and can even make experiences that will last a lifetime. Because my dad said those wise words, I no longer see celebrations as just customs, but as things that really mean something. They're great chances to enjoy the moment, be joyful, and be grateful for what you have and the people you are with. Taking into account the above celebrations, I'm proud of having made the path of life worth it. Thank you very much to my dad for telling me these wise words: "The purpose of life is a life of purpose" by Robin Sharma. They helped me value every moment of my life and the feelings that festivals bring out in people.

Stories and lessons from key festivals

Festivals have always been a big part of my life since I grew up in an Indian home. Our family got together for every holiday, which brought us closer together and made us happy. The three pieces in my dad's book called "Happiness: How, When, and Why" really helped me form my thoughts on those cultural celebrations. Festivals are more than just rituals; they tell us stories about life, its lessons, and the customs we share. They show us how important it is to be happy, thankful, and together, even when things are small. We love Diwali, which means "festival of lights," more than any other holiday. Adding joy, hope, and goodness to our lives is what Diwali is all about, not just lighting up their homes with lamps and firecrackers. My dad would sometimes talk about how Diwali was when he was a kid. My grandfather told me my dad was very naughty! Then he told stories about how he made up stories about doing terrible things like stealing sugar from the kitchen and setting off fireworks before it was time, among other things. Not only were these stories fun to read, but they also taught me the phrase that "wealth does not equal happiness."

Somehow, these events helped us remember the history and customs of our people, which seemed like another benefit. They were a way for people to pass on cultural beliefs and ways of life from one family to the next. "What makes us very special? was something my dad would say over and over. No matter how much we have accomplished, "Our ability to share what we know, irrespective of our level of achievements," reminds us of how important it is to record and share our traditional knowledge. I learnt that festivals help us connect with our roots, learn about our history, and be proud of who we are. Fun events and parties like festivals are a big part of making people and communities happy. They bring people together, encourage unity, and create experiences that last a lifetime. All the holiday information my dad gave me has helped me understand why and how these events are celebrated. These events give us chances to enjoy life, be grateful for what we have, and meet important people. My dad told us that it's okay to hug each other, think about life, and get our energy back in these situations. I was able to learn a lot about life from the holidays that I grew up knowing, such as Christmas, Diwali, Holi, Eid and even Navratri. Some of the things that are learnt are sharing, acceptance, kindness, and realising how useful it is to exist.

This I was once told by my father: "Festivals are the threads that weave the fabric of our cultural and spiritual identity." This has been very helpful as I journey through life. These celebrations do not only create honour but also make people happy and satisfied in their lives. We should enjoy these occasions and share them with the people that we hold dear to us. It remains rather important for individuals to be happy all year since that is always the key way through which people advance in life.

Chapter 10

The Significance of Duty and Responsibility

Responsibility and duty hold great significance within Indian society. They are interwoven into every aspect of our day-to-day existence. "कमज़ोर इंसान सचाई का साथ कभी दे नहीं सकता और कायर इंसान उसूलों को कभी निभा नहीं सकता," These rules, which are otherwise referred to as the "Dharma," serve as our moral codes, faith, and societal norms. My dad wrote a book called "Happiness: How, When, and Why" which is a much deeper exploration of what it means to have a duty and therefore responsibility. It demonstrates how they can assist people to be joyful and maintain harmony in their homes and the larger world. Reflecting on the lessons that he teaches, and the knowledge of intellectuals assists me in recalling that, it is not wrong to understand and perform duties as they make us find meaning and happiness in life.

Understanding the Concept of 'Dharma' in Our Culture

In the sphere of ethics, where it is used as a reference to duty, fairness, and order, the word is just as important to Indian culture and thought as it is to the ethics field. "Dharma," my dad used to say, means a person's rights and duties in a certain situation, like as a father, a son, a neighbour, or a community member. In the Bhagavad Gita, Lord Krishna said, "It is better to do one's own duty improperly than to do someone else's duty well." That's what he'd say. "Dharma," which means "that which is right," is the subject of this lesson.

His usual comments are phrases like 'Gandhi once said, The best way to find yourself is to lose yourself in the service of others.' In this quotation, it says that we should never act in our own self-interest and that has been explained very well. His use of the quote by Swami Vivekananda – 'Arise, awake, and stop not till the aim is achieved,' highlights the fact that it is time to be serious about the tasks at hand. The term "dharma" is of ancient Indian origin and has been employed in literature and mythology. My family members told me stories and lessons from the epics of Mahabharata and Ramayana. The best person to be obeying the law was Lord Rama, and my dad would tell stories using him most of the time. This story taught me about "Dharma," which means that you have to do something even if you don't want to or even if it's hard. Fixing what's wrong is what it's about, not making things easy for oneself.

"Dharma" is used in our society to correct people and teach them how to live a good life, especially in the family. "Dharma" for parents means more than just feeding the family and meeting their basic wants. It also means taking care of their child's character and soul. He used to say, "a parent's duty is to lay the foundation for their children's future, both in terms of character and knowledge." This fits with the usual idea that parents are the best people to teach their kids right from wrong.

For kids, Dharma means listening to their parents, doing well in school, and helping out around the house and with family events. He always told me, "Respect for one's parents and elders is the first step towards understanding one's duties." Honouring parents or older people doesn't just mean following their rules, which is also known as being afraid of them. It also means recognising their knowledge and power in the family.

People have seen that if the ideas of "dharma" are followed, there will be order and peace in the home. Every member of the family should take care of their own duties so that everyone can do their jobs in an honest way. My dad says that this is the kind of setting that keeps the family in order and peace. "The family is as smooth as a machine whose parts are all perfectly intertwined," he would say a lot of the time.

The Significance of Duty and Responsibility in Family Life

In Indian homes, duty and responsibility are the two most important ideals that keep things stable and in order. They help make sure that everyone in the family is treated equally and, with everyone's help, make sure that everyone is healthy. One thing my dad taught me was that "a family is a tree, and each member is a branch. If each branch does its job, the tree grows strong."

One thing that contributes to this kind of unity is that everyone in the family knows exactly what their job is. Parents are supposed to provide the most money and spiritual guidance, while kids are supposed to do things like study, do chores, etc. "A family is productive when everyone knows their job and does it well," my dad always said. Putting tasks into groups like this helps the family meet its goals and makes everyone feel good about the work they do.

Each family member's duties also help the family as a whole. "A family is strong when its members are united and willing to work together for the good of all," my dad used to say. Family members will get along and value each other if they do their jobs.

The Role of Duty in Personal Fulfillment

Due to this, duty and obligation are more than just doing things; they give our lives meaning and joy. The main idea of the book my dad wrote is that when someone works hard and honestly at something, they feel full. As he once said, "The greatest happiness I know is to work for an idea I believe in and do it as well as I can." For parents, doing their jobs, like making money for the family and taking care of their kids, is the best prize and the key to happiness. "The success of a parent is not the amount of wealth they accumulate, but the kind of people they bring out of the children," my dad always said. When someone is a good caretaker, they know that the value of their work can't be judged in the short term, but in the long term. This quote brings out that idea. Children also feel proud and happy when they do their jobs at home or school. "Children learn to work hard and feel like they belong when they have their own roles and responsibilities," my dad always said. In terms of personal growth, this is very important.

The Foundation of Family Harmony

One way to look at it is that duty and responsibility are what keep the family calm. This is because when everyone in the family knows their job and follows it, it brings the family closer together and helps them. As my dad always said, "A family that works together stays together." This may be an overused saying, but it's really true.

Duty not only keeps the peace, but it also makes sure that everyone acts in a way that is good for the family. "This feeling of being together is what makes a family happy," my dad frequently stated. "When everyone in the family looks out for each other, even if it's not always convenient." This is why the family stays together even when bad things happen.

The Moral Imperative of 'Dharma'

Also, "Dharma" isn't just about doing things; it's also about being responsible and ethical. Paying attention to one's duties is important, but doing so in the right way is even more important. "Duty without morality is like a body without a soul," my dad always said. For this reason, we should do our jobs properly and avoid getting blood on our hands from innocent people.

For parents, this moral duty means not only taking care of the family's basic wants but also teaching their kids right from wrong and religion. My dad always said, "A parent's most important job is to be a good example for their kids." This means that a parent shouldn't just tell their kids what's right; they should also do it themselves so that their kids can see how to do it.

Kids also need to do their part. They need to show respect for adults, work hard in school to get good grades and help run the home. Regarding respect and responsibility, my dad always said, "Respect and responsibility go hand in hand. If kids learn to respect adults, they won't have to be told to do their jobs." This kind of respect is a big part of "Dharma," and the family needs it to keep going smoothly.

Responsibility and Performance of Duties as a Pathway to Meaning and Satisfaction

In other words, performing duties is more than just doing your job; it's also a way of giving your life value. It was clear from what my dad taught me that we find the most value in our lives when we do our jobs honestly and with integrity. He always said, "Happiness makes the best work done out of love and sincerity taste better." This duty brings happiness to parents since it is their responsibility to nurture and prepare their children for the future. If they fulfil this duty, they will become happy. According to my father, the only sensation that could potentially be considered rewarding for a parent is the feeling that comes with the knowledge that everything has been done to ensure that your family is being cared for and directed in the appropriate manner.

As they fulfil their obligations, the youngsters are also afforded the opportunity to experience the same sense of pride and fulfilment. Children should be encouraged to work hard, according to my father, who taught me that when children are raised to realise that it is good to work hard, then they will be proud of themselves for the rest of their lives. He taught me this philosophy when I was growing up.

Strengthening Bonds Through the Fulfillment of Duties

Fulfilling tasks not only makes one feel good, but they also help family members get along better. This means that once everyone has done their part, there is always a shared understanding, trust, and respect, which is necessary for any family to work. My dad always said, "A family is strong when they stick together, and sticking together comes from being responsible."

An important way that tasks strengthen family ties is by making everyone feel like they have a responsibility to each other. My dad thought that if everyone in the family did what they were supposed to do, then everyone would understand each other and stick together through good times and bad. But above all, Dad told me to believe the words of Gurudev Sri Sri Ravi Shankar, the famous quote "It is only through inner silence that you can bring out happiness and celebration in life."

Collective Happiness Through the Performance of Duties

The performance of tasks isn't just about doing what one's supposed to do; it's also a key part of making parents happy and successful. That shows that when everyone in the family does their job right, it leads to respect and unity in relationships and in the family. "Happiness is not something you chase alone; it is something you chase together," my dad used to say.

The realisation of this collective happiness occurs when every member of the family is content and is actively contributing to the happiness of all the other members of the family. It is always better to put the needs of the family ahead of your own because it brings the family closer together, my dad once told me.

To sum up, duty and obligation are big parts of our lives. When I think about what my dad taught me, I believe that those ideas are the keys to happiness, loving relationships, and a healthy society. The notion of 'Dharma,' which refers to the duties and obligations that individuals have in their families, whether as parents or children or in society, offers people a sense of fulfilment in their life and helps to direct their behaviour.

It is important to remember that responsibility, like duty, is not just a drag; it's a way to plan our lives and find meaning, happiness, and fulfilment. We need to be honest, and dedicated, and feel responsible to our families and community in the work we do. A long time ago, my dad said, "The world is a better place for everyone when everyone does their job with love and truth." With this in mind, let us always remember that our duties and obligations are what make life worth living.

Chapter 11

The Art of Giving and Charity

In India, daan is more than just giving money or time to someone in need. It is a way of life that is respected because it is based on spiritual and moral principles that many families and Indian society uphold. As a child, my dad always told me that giving is not only a good thing to do, but it's also an important part of life that will make one happy, fulfilled, and generally happy. He would always say this to me: "अगर आप किसी की मदद करने में सक्षम हैं, और आपने किसी की मदद नहीं की, तो समझें आपने जीवन में कुछ नहीं किया:" which means, "If you have the power to help others and don't, then you haven't lived your life." This section is mostly about talking about generosity in the social spreading of happiness, its part in creating the reward (which I describe with the help of my dad), and the useful information I got from many people.

Cultural Tradition: The Roots of Daan

As the people of India call it, "Daan," charity is not a new idea; it has been around since the beginning of time. Becoming responsible for this is a big job that is often religious and moral in nature. A quote from one of the holy books that my dad said was "Daanam Niyamam Sadaiva," which means "Charity is a perpetual virtue." In Indian society today, many people still think this way about the importance of giving and the good things that happen when people follow the social norm of giving. As a result of what was discovered, the act of giving cannot be reduced to the simple act of donating anything;

rather, it also requires making changes that improve the lives of other individuals.

His words helped me remember that it wasn't just me who should do it, but the whole family. As he said, "What matters is not how much money a family makes but how much they spend on others." I was taught to give. For example, people are told to help others because it's seen as an honour to be able to do so. Another trait that is passed down from one generation to the next is generosity, which in turn helps to cultivate a culture of caring, which includes being aware of the problems that other people are facing and embracing the culture of giving.

Family Values: The Role of Giving in Moral Upbringing

In Indian families, through giving it is believed that one is able to impart moral and ethical lessons in the society. This is because these young people are brought up with the virtues of sharing, helping others and being charitable. When I was with my dad, he would always tell me, "A child who learns to give grows up to be an adult who values giving." I made sure to follow the lesson. We learnt that our actions could make someone else's life better by doing things like giving our toys to kids who didn't have any and doing charity things.

My dad taught me that the most important thing in life is to be ready to give, not money but something of great value. He was very proud of the Bhagavad Gita, in which Lord Krishna says, "It is better to do your duty and not worry about the results of your actions." In a way, this is also true for "Daan." According to my dad, real giving is when someone does something without expecting anything in return and with the specific goal of making other people happy and the world run smoothly.

Social Responsibility: Charity as a Collective Act

In India, the idea of kindness isn't just about helping oneself; it's also about taking care of one's family or kin. Giving to charity is another way for families to help others. They can give food, clothes, or even money to people who need it. My dad used to believe that acts like these bring family members closer together and strengthen the morals that hold the family together. "Charity begins at home," he would always say. Much can be learnt from this saying, especially about how it applies to families staying together.

My dad also insisted on regular charity and was shocked that it could only be done on certain days. He always said, "Every day is a chance to be kind; this makes you more likely to do nice things every day." As a child, my parents always set aside some of our money to help people in need. This change happened not only in how much money we gave, but also in how many hours we gave to help others. People learnt that caring about other people's well-being isn't something that can be done just once by donating things to a nearby shelter or cleaning up their neighbourhood. My dad used to tell us stories about Karna, who is known for giving more than anyone else. Despite the many problems Karna had in his life, he was always willing to help people who asked. I learnt from this story that kindness comes from the heart and that helping others is its own prize.

Daan: Charitable Giving and Its Effects on Happiness in a Cultural Context

Daan, often known as charity, is a method of providing assistance and support to other people, while simultaneously contributing to the improvement of the overall morale and happiness of those who make donations. People in India believe that "Daan" is a holy act that cleanses the giver's soul and helps them reach spiritual freedom. People who give are also those who receive, my dad used to say. It is said that when people give, they also receive, which helps the mental side of making themselves happy.

Giving was a good thing that happened in our family and made everyone happy and satisfied. Since I was a little child, if my father wanted to give me a toy or some other kind of gift, he would always tell me that it is not the act of giving that is important, but rather the emotions that are being produced by the people who are receiving the gift. "That is true happiness when one has helped change the lives of many," he said at one point. This was especially clear when families did volunteer work during religious and cultural events. Giving the poor rice, sweets, and other things during Diwali or new clothes during Eid or any other holiday was more satisfying than having all the things you could want.

Personal Testimonies and the Nature of Rewards from Giving

Some people say that receiving is better than giving, and I agree with them. There are so many good things that happen when you give. As for these effects, my dad used to talk to me about the spiritual benefits of giving, which are generally thought of as good feelings like joy, happiness, and satisfaction. "The joy of giving is the joy of living" was a saying that he would always remember. That is, giving is the only way to really feel this joy. I will never forget what my dad said in his story. Often, he thinks back to a time when he was a child or teen and volunteered at the local orphanage on the weekends. He talked about it as one of the best times of his life. He would enthusiastically say, "I think the happiest moment would be seeing the kids' faces light up with happiness." This taught him that giving is valuable because it changes other people's lives, not because of the reward one gets in return.

People in Indian homes who get money tend to feel very happy when they give it to others. This fulfilment, then, goes hand in hand with inner peace and personal satisfaction, since people meet the wants of each person. "The heart that gives is always a heart that is full," was something my dad used to say. This just means that giving has many perks, one of which is making people feel good. In addition to the mental benefits, doing good things for others guarantees that they will be recognised or respected more in the community. Family members who are kind are seen as decent by society, which helps their standing in it. "Respect brings respect, and you don't earn it with money. You earn it by doing good things for other people," my dad used to say. The idea behind this knowledge is that acts of kindness have social benefits because they make the person who does them look better in the eyes of others.

Spiritual Rewards: The Deeper Impact of Giving

Most likely, the most important benefits are those that have to do with spirituality. Another theme that comes up a lot in personal stories is the feeling of change, like a shift in the person's faith or general view of the world. My dad once said that being kind can bring you closer to God. "Daan is the way to attain moksha," a quote from the old texts, would be used by him. In Indian culture, these words are deeply rooted. People think that charity cleans the soul and builds good karma.

These feelings were shown to me by my dad's own giving experiences, and they would later shape how he gave in the future. He used to say that some of the good things he did for other people, especially when he did them freely, gave him happiness that money could not buy. The thing I heard him say most often was, "Charity was the mirror through which a man's soul could be purified." Several religious beliefs back up this idea. One definition of charity is an act done from the heart without expecting anything in return.

Positive Ripple Effect: The Collective Impact of Giving

They thought that helping the community get ahead was one of the best things about giving. My dad said more than once that giving should inspire people to give to a good cause, which would lead to more donations to charity. For example, he might say, "One act of kindness can spark a chain reaction of giving." At its core, this idea is total charity, which means that every act of kindness has the power to make the world a better place.

In our neighbourhood, it was normal to see someone doing something nice for someone else, which inspired other people to do the same. Kind acts, like a family giving a meal to an animal shelter or a group of people having a charity event for a cause, brought more people to the event. Giving, as my dad often said, "germinates through the hearts of the givers and the recipients." I think this means that helping doesn't just help the person who does it; it also helps other people in society, which makes everyone happier.

Embracing the Art of Giving

Finally, it's important to note that giving gifts and being kind were big parts of Indian culture for the principles of Karmakanda and Daan. Thinking about it more, all my dad has taught me is that being kind isn't a chore, but a good thing that can give your life meaning, happiness, and even satisfaction. It is clear that the saying "दान से धर्म की प्राप्ति होती है," (charity brings justice) is true when you think about the benefits of "data". This shows how important it is to give; it changes and helps people's lives, both the source and the receiver. It also spreads good vibes throughout a community and even further if done by a group.

Thinking about what my dad taught me about giving has made me think more about charity and happiness. Indeed, giving is more than just a way to get things. It's also a way to embrace the best qualities in ourselves and others, like kindness, caring, and selflessness. "Rather than focussing on charity as an activity, a better approach is to look at the love and intention behind it," my beloved father suggested. Now is the time to really live these lessons, to make giving and being kind a part of who we are, and to find true happiness in this.

Chapter 12

Health and Well-Being

Being healthy is therefore a part of having a balanced life. India believes that taking care of one's health includes their physical, mental, and even spiritual well-being. With the help of my father's stories and Ayurveda, I now understand health and well-being in this way. This chapter will talk about Ayurveda, the Indian approach to health and wellness, and the moral concept of "Dharma." These personal thoughts about health and energy were inspired by the book my dad wrote and what experts know. "Yoga is not only exercising the body; it also exercises the mind," my dad would say. You can stay physically and mentally fit through yoga by doing asanas and breathing.

Holistic Health in Indian Households

Indian families take a broader view of health, taking into account the physical, mental, and spiritual parts of life. My dad always said that health isn't just not having any sicknesses, but having the best possible physical, mental, and spiritual well-being. "Health is wealth, and it's true that nothing is more important than health," he would say. This way of thought can be seen in the everyday things people do, their focus on family, and their push for prevention, all of which are important parts of Indian culture. He often used quotes from Swami Vivekananda. One that stands out to me is, "Meditation can turn fools into sages, but alas, fools never meditate."

Daily Routines: The Foundation of Well-Being

Thus, it can be said that daily habits play a big role in general health every day. In our family, doing things like going for a walk in the morning, doing yoga, eating right, and reciting spiritual verses became habits. In the past, my dad believed that these habits were the key to living a good life. He often said, "Once discipline is set in the morning, the day flows smoothly from there." Not only did the morning walk help the body, it also helped the soul. Yoga and meditation were also planned and practiced every day. "Yoga is the journey of the self, through the self, to the self," my father used to say when he talked about how important it was to do yoga for mental and physical health. Yoga, flexibility, and strength training complete the physical package, and meditation calms the mind.

Ensuring we ate well-balanced meals was another part of the day plan. Food was medicine, according to my dad, and everything we ate was as fresh as possible. Meals made with local ingredients and spices like ginger, turmeric, and cumin were especially special. These foods were presented healthily and had all the nutrients that the body and mind needed.

Family-Centric Care: A Collective Responsibility

People in Indian society, especially family members, are responsible for the health of everyone in the family as a whole. This means that everyone is responsible for their health. One thing my dad taught us is that everyone's health is important. "A healthy family is a happy family," he would say, and he would make sure that everyone was healthy. Another thing that stood out was the focus on the family-centred approach to health problems. Paying attention to each other's health was a normal part of family life, whether it was going for a walk in the morning or taking medicine for a cold that might have come on. Everyone in the family was involved, which made the whole thing work together to keep everyone healthy and happy.

Preventive Focus: The Key to Longevity

Indian families understand and practice preventive care. He always told my mother that it is better to stop an illness before it starts than to treat it after it's happened. This was especially true when it came to food, exercise, and traditional practices. He would think of the saying "An ounce of prevention is better than a pound of cure," which meant that people should take care of their health before they get sick instead of waiting until they are sick to get better. This preventive focus affected my family. Exercise, good dieting, and health management strategies like turmeric for inflammation and honey ginger for colds were common in our home. These precautions not only kept us healthy, but they also made us more aware of and responsible for our health.

Indian Practices for Health and Wellness

It is an Indian practice, and the main goal of Ayurveda is to keep the body and spirit in balance. Some of these practices are yoga, meditation, natural cures, eating healthy foods, and mind practices that help the body stay healthy. The changes of the seasons and their cleaning rituals were also good for our family's health as a whole. My dad told me that these things clean a person up and get them ready for what each season has to give. For example, some of these detox methods involved not eating for a certain amount of time, drinking herbal teas, and doing certain yoga poses. That's why my dad liked to say, "Detoxification is the beginning of the rejuvenation process."

Don't forget that being active is also a big part of our daily lives. My dad wanted us to do a lot of different things, from traditional games like Kabaddi and Kho-Kho to more modern ones like cycling, swimming, and so on. He believed that working out was good for both the body and the mind. He also liked to tell us of the Hindi proverb, "स्वास्थ्य सबसे बड़ी संपत्ति है," which means that being healthy is the only way to be rich.

Yoga and Meditation: The Pillars of Wellness

Indian culture has always included yoga and meditation because they are good for the body and mind. My dad always told me that doing things like that could lead to change. People used to say, "Yoga makes the body healthy, meditation makes the mind healthy, and doing both makes the soul healthy as well."

Yoga is one of these practices that plays a big role in Indian health care. It is based on controlled breathing, certain body positions, and meditation. My dad used to say that yoga isn't just a way to work out, it's a way of life. Quotes were his favourite. "Yoga is not about touching your toes; it's what you learn on the way down." What this saying says about the benefits of yoga is that they are both physical and social.

People thought that meditation, on the other hand, brought peace and order to the mind. In two easy words, my dad could explain what meditation was: "the art of silencing the mind." He thought that practising every day made people less stressed, more focused, and more mentally stable. From what their parents told them, every family should do meditation every day.

Home Remedies: The Wisdom of Tradition

Home medicines are also a big part of health care in India. The ideas behind these home cures come from Ayurveda and have been used for decades to treat minor illnesses without having to go to the doctor.

What my dad thought about the saying "nature is the best healer" was very true. He used natural medicines like honey, turmeric, ginger, and neem to show this. We also paid close attention to how much water we drank because we wanted to stay as healthy as possible. My dad always told us, "पानी पीने का सही समय है सुबह उठते ही," which means "It's best to drink water first thing in the morning." Another custom was to drink one glass of warm water first thing in the morning to clean out the intestines and get rid of waste.

For example, turmeric was often used to treat inflammation, and honey and ginger were often used to treat a cold or cough. His words stuck with me: "The kitchen is our pharmacy." He meant that we used natural remedies to stay healthy and treat most of our everyday illnesses. In fact, these home remedies not only worked, they also showed how smart our ancestors were.

Balanced Diet: Nourishing the Body and Mind

In India, food has always been seen as an important factor in determining health and well-being. "You are what you eat" was something my dad always believed, so that's how the food in our house was made. We used to eat well-balanced meals made with fresh, seasonal foods and spices that were good for you.

The food we ate not only filled up our tanks, but it also made our bodies healthy in general. For instance, when I was a kid, my dad would say things like, "A balanced diet is the basis of a balanced life." For all meals to be nutritious and tasty, the above probably influenced how they were prepared.

Mental Health Practices: Nurturing the Mind

As in other practices, psychological well-being also occupies a central place in Indian practices. Some practices include breath control (pranayama), mindfulness, and frequent religious practices aimed at keeping mental and emotional health in check. My father used to say that "a healthy mind is the basis of a healthy life."

Another part of the daily routine in our home was Pranayama or breath control. He once mentioned to me, "Take control of your breath, and you control your mind." This was used to find stillness of the mind, stress relief, and focused attention. It is worth noting that apart from pranayama, the concept of mindfulness was also introduced as a means of avoiding distractions and keeping the mind focused.

Daily prayers and other religious activities formed the core of many of the programs aimed at maintaining mental health. My father was a firm advocate for 'the soul also needs exercise', which these practices accorded to the mind, enabling one to feel at ease and fulfilled.

The Role of the Ayurveda Lifestyle and Process

Ancient Indians have used Ayurveda to improve people's health and well-being for a very long time. The goal is to keep the body's three forces (Vata, Pitta, and Kapha) in the right balance. My dad used to say, "Ayurveda is the science of life and knowledge of longevity."

The body's doshas are said to be healthy when they are in balance and unity with each other. People used the saying "balance is the key to health" to talk about their health because my dad believed it. Ayurveda says that it is very important to know and understand your body and choose foods and exercises that work with it.

For example, if someone has a Vata dominating type, they might feel anxious and dry, but Ayurveda says that they should eat warm foods that are high in oil because of this. That was something my dad always told me: "Listen to your body and it will tell you what it needs." Due to this idea, Ayurveda is used to make the body work better.

Daily Rituals (Dinacharya) and Seasonal Adjustments (Ritucharya): A Routine for Health with Harmony with Nature

As part of some of the processes, people follow Dinacharya, which are daily habits or activities that help them get or stay healthy. A few of these practices are pulling out the tongue, using oil, and drinking warm water first thing in the morning to help clean the body. They were a part of our daily lives because my dad always said, "A disciplined routine leads to a healthy life." For example, oil pulling was done in the morning to clean the mouth and keep it healthy. "Wash your face and brush your teeth when you wake up, and your thoughts will be clean too," my dad always said. Tongue scraping was another way to clean the mouth early in the morning and get rid of germs.

Ayurveda also stresses following certain rules for eating and living based on the season. These rules are called Ritucharya. One thing my dad always said that was true about how we took care of our health: "Nature is our best teacher." In Ayurveda, one of the most important things my father always stressed was the "dinacharya," or daily routine. He taught us that we needed to stick to a daily routine to keep the three subtle forces (Vata, Pitta, and Kapha) in our bodies in balance. Every morning, sesame oil was used for "oil pulling," which was meant to clean the body and keep teeth clean. After this, "abhyanga," or oil massage with warm plant oils, was done. This relaxed the muscles and improved blood flow, both of which helped the body get rid of toxins.

According to Ayurveda, people should eat warm and hot foods in the winter, which is controlled by the Kapha dosha, to help their bodies deal with the cold and damp weather. That being said, during the summer, when the Pitta dosha rules, foods like cucumber and mint are recommended because they are thought to cool the body. "Honour the seasons," my dad once told me, "and you will stay healthy." These examples show how we should act when the weather changes.

Herbal Remedies: The Power of Nature

Every meal was made from scratch every day with fresh, seasonal, and locally grown food that also had Ayurvedic qualities, like turmeric, cumin, and coriander. When it came to diet, he believed that food should bring everyone's doshas back into balance. For example, foods that were warm, moist, and nutritious were best for Vata types, while foods that were cooling and regulating were best for Pitta types. Ayurveda uses plant mixtures and natural chemicals to help people stay healthy for a long time. "Nature gives us everything we need to stay healthy," my dad used to say all the time. That's why we used plants like ashwagandha for stress, neem for body cleansing, and triphala for digestion.

As an example, ashwagandha was once used to lower worry and boost energy. Ashwagandha is the herb of power, my dad would often tell me. "It makes you strong mentally and physically," he would say. Neem was another herb that was used to clean the body and improve the look of skin. Triphala was another popular herb for treating indigestion. In addition to being natural, these drugs worked well and showed that nature could be used to keep people healthy.

Spiritual and Mental Health: The Heart of Ayurveda

Ayurveda considers soul and mind health while assessing total wellness. My dad thought the mind controlled the body. Because of this, he taught us to care for our bodies and minds. In Ayurveda, we meditated, were positive, and kept our surroundings clean. For example, to clear their minds of worry and other kinds of pressure, the people in the study meditated and limited the kinds of thoughts they had. He would say things like, "The mind is in charge of the body, and a healthy mind means healthy living." It was also important to keep the peace; they think that "home is a place to find peace of mind." Indian health care considers body, mind, and spirit to assess health. I discuss how my father and Ayurveda have shaped my overall health and fitness philosophy from this perspective. Ayurveda taught us to meditate, stay positive, and be hygienic.

My father gave me these health and happiness standards, which I still follow. They encourage individuals to take responsibility, understand that a quiet and healthy existence is attainable, practice preventive care, and value nature. Because of this, my dad was right when he said, "Health is not just the absence of disease; it is a state of perfect physical, mental, social, and spiritual well-being, with all forms of moderation." The spirit of these important principles should share the idea and secrets of living a healthy and happy life with everyone.

Chapter 13

Finding Purpose through Work

The Concept of 'Karma Yoga' (Selfless Work) and Its Importance

Karma Yoga was a common topic of conversation in my Indian-themed home where I grew up. My dad, always said that work isn't just for making money; it's for reaching a lifelong objective. In Indian culture, this goal includes more than just getting ahead for oneself; it also includes helping others and family. My dad didn't say many words, but the ones he did say were deep. For example, he would say, "Work is a form of worship when done with love and devotion."

It's important to note that in India, work is seen as a job where people try to figure out what their life's meaning is. Not only does it help people find jobs, but it also points them in the direction of achieving their goals and being happy. My dad would always say that work ethic is very important in our family and that things can only be done with focus and determination. He always told me, "Success is the byproduct of relentless dedication and an unwavering commitment to one's duties." I remember that. This particular piece of advice has changed how I work and how I see my work as a gift to society.

The Bhagavad Gita talks about different types of yoga. Karma Yoga stresses the idea of not caring about yourself. It says that the only way to get real pleasure is to work without caring about the results. My dad always told me this verse: "कर्मण्येवातिकारस्ते मा फलेषु कदाचन," which means that someone can do their job but can't demand what will happen as a result. This thought stuck with me and shaped how I thought about work, putting more value on the process than the outcome.

In our home, Karma Yoga was done by doing all of our chores and tasks around the house. People didn't see these chores as just work; they saw them as ways to help the family and others. My dad told me, "Perform your duty with devotion, not for recognition, but for the fulfilment it brings." With this approach, I learnt that every job is important, no matter how small. There was always a focus on service and responsibility, whether it was doing chores around the house or helping out with neighbourhood projects.

By connecting to faith, Karma Yoga also helped to bring work and life together. Most Indians see their job as a spiritual practice in and of itself. For them, work is all about practising some kind of discipline, ethics, or moral duty. This way of putting together work-life faith was a big idea for me. Some time ago, my dad told me that we can work better and feel less stressed when we don't care about how our actions turn out. "Attachment creates stress," he would say. "Detachment brings peace and clarity." Life lessons like this are useful whether one is dealing with problems with other people or at work.

Tales of Personal Success and Happiness as a Result of an Individual's Career

My dad told me stories of his own success and happiness to show me the family values he believed in. One of these was Karma Yoga. These weren't just stories of people going from nothing to having a lot of money; they were journeys to reach their goals and dreams of becoming great professionals. My dad always told me stories about men who got ahead in life because they were focused, dedicated, and committed to their work.

A family friend who became a doctor was one of the most read stories. She had a rough ride; she ran into a lot of problems along the way, like not having enough money or time to study, among other things. Even so, she was dedicated to her job and wanted to help others, which drove her. "Success is not the amount of money you make, but the number of lives you touch," my father often told her. He admired how dedicated she was to helping others. Hearing this story helped me realise how important it is to give instead of get.

Another story that comes to mind quickly is about a woman from our neighbourhood who used her love of cooking to start a food business. Even with all of these problems, she worked hard and built a successful business that made her feel good about herself. "Follow your passion, and passion will lead you to purpose," my dad always told me. These words inspired me to be as dedicated to my hobbies as I am now because doing what you love is what makes you successful.

The people in the above Karma Yoga success stories have given their work more meaning and significance and are happier at work as a result. My dad always said that being happy with your job doesn't just mean making money; it also means loving what you do. When someone's work shows their beliefs and helps a good cause, he would say, "Work is an enhancement to life and not a burden." It was these words that helped me figure out how I felt about work as a way to advance my job and myself.

From personal memories, I know that my father put a lot of value on family pride or the happiness that comes from a loved one's success. Indian culture says that success is not just about one person, but about the whole group. When a family member does something great in life, it's always a happy and proud moment. "Your success is not only yours but also the success of your family," my dad would always tell me. It's even more important to know that success doesn't just mean winning for yourself; it also means winning for those who helped you or added to your success.

Finding Purpose through Work

With these lessons in mind, I now understand that going to work to make money is not enough. People who do this have strong beliefs, a sense of purpose, and a strong connection to their work, the community, and the act of serving. People in India see work as a way to fulfil their life's goals and help their family and society. This view comes from the idea that "hard work pays off" and that people who are dedicated and work hard are likely to be successful and happy. This has shaped how I work so that I can get a better return on my efforts in the future.

When combined with faith in the right way, work can be a great way to heal. Most Indians see their jobs as more than just work. They see them as a trip, even a pilgrimage, where they can improve their self-control, professionalism, and morality. My life philosophy is that work should be more than just a way to make money; it should also be spiritual. This has helped me pursue my job with passion and dedication.

Karma yoga has helped me take control of how I think about work and what it's all for the most. Through helping others and taking my job seriously and properly, I've learnt that the benefits of work aren't material gains but making a difference for a good cause. Another thing that karma yoga has helped me understand is that I shouldn't care about the effects of my work. Now I work with more focus and less stress.

So, karma yoga is a way to learn about doing good work, and it has changed the way people think about work and duty in society for the better. This is another way that Karma Yoga has helped me understand that it's not the end results that make us happy at work, but the work itself. My father told me stories about people who were successful and happy in their own lives, which helped me believe that having a job doesn't mean making a lot of money; it means being happy while doing your job. These insights will stay with me as I move forward, and I'm sure they will help me find a job that gives me meaning and satisfaction. In the end, it's not just the job that pays the bills; it's also the trip to find value and purpose in life.

Chapter 14

The Legacy of Resilience and Service

A Life Marked by Challenges and Unyielding Spirit

There were hard times and good times in his life. Every stitch in the fabric of life told a story about his strength and character. To sum up, things that could have made a man afraid or careful became the foundations of his strong and happy personality from a young age.

What happened was the first and scariest of these events. One day, my dad leaned against the balcony rail on the second floor because he was interested in the music. He lost his balance and hit the ground. Lucky for him, there were no major injuries, but he did get a few small cuts on his head. The accident, which could have ended terribly, could have been a sign for him about how important it is to get back up after falling in life.

On the second occasion, it happened during a family vacation. Even though my dad was very enthusiastic, he liked to play, so he stood at the back of the car while Grandpa drove it back to the road. He fell and hit his head on the car because of some jerk. He triumphed through the attack with only minor injuries, even though he was not scared. Another thing that the man showed at this time was self-reliance, which would become more noticeable over the next few years.

Until he was a teenager, he still liked to try new things. The next big adventure began when my dad chose to check out his uncle's car, which seemed to have a smell of smoke around it. A single moment of curiosity to grab a match caused him to start a little fire, even though he had no intention of doing so. It was hard for him to breathe inside, but thank God he was able to get out without much problem. Because he thought life was meant to be hard and met with bravery and endurance, this event didn't make him change his mind.

I felt physically and emotionally moved by these events, which served as a lesson that life is full of surprises, but happiness lies in overcoming the expected. My dad didn't stop having adventures when he was young; he still had a lot of them when he was a youngster. As he was moving into his new home, he walked around the yard and tripped and fell down the marble stairs. By the time he got to the nose, he was too hurt to continue. A scar from a stitch can still be seen today. It was amazing how he just got up and started dancing like nothing was wrong. That was a sign of self-control. This response says everything about his personality: the subject's ability to be happy even when bad things happen.

The Philosophy of Selfless Service

So, even though my dad had a lot of problems in his personal life, he never shut himself off from society. Instead, they seemed to motivate him to help people in need, which was a core concept he never wavered from. He loved talking about the three types of charity, which are called Mansa, Vacha, and Karmna. These mean physical, speech, and mental clarity, respectively. His ideas were clear: when you talk about charity, it's not just about having lots of stuff; it's also about what you do with your heart, your words, and your hands.

According to these practices, one should put aside their own wants in order to help others. For example, he signed to donate his eyes, kidneys, and lungs to other people after he died. At this point, things were not going as planned; this showed how much he cared about a cause bigger than himself and his age.

But my dad's charity wasn't just about spending a lot of money. He believed that a person's total facial expressions showed that they were kind. Everyone he met was nice to him, and he always put others first and tried to do things that helped other people in some way.

One of these stories was about our old driver. My dad saw that the driver was always late, so he asked the driver what was going on. Needless to say, an example can be provided by an experience with our old driver, with whom we often witnessed this. I recall my father asking the man politely one day why he always arrived after work hours, observing that he was late most of the time. The driver said that most of the time he had to wake up early in the morning, take a bus, and then cover a long distance on foot and this was sometimes time-consuming. In particular, in case of any difficulty, without any second thought, my father arranged to buy him a used bike to alleviate the burden. My father made the driver promise not to tell anyone about this and this was an aspect of my father's humility and his caring nature towards other people. The kind of person my dad was—the kind who helps and cares for others without expecting anything in return.

I saw him sign up to help at the local food banks when fear and uncertainty were at an all-time high at the start of the COVID-19 outbreak. Whatever the case, he knew that poor people living in rural places were suffering a lot from hunger. He also got four of his colleagues to work together to make and serve food in shifts. The program started with fifty meals a day, but as more people signed up, it grew to 500 meals a day. My dad didn't want to be in the spotlight.

He cared more about how this work could help people who are in need and hunger.

The Power of Resilience and Gratitude

My father was able to show his perseverance not just in times of physical danger, but also in other situations as well. It was something he was born with and taught himself throughout his life. The man showed that happiness is not having any problems, but having light when things are dark. The way he dealt with both small and big problems in his life showed that he believed this.

Another touching example of my father's kind-heartedness is the fact that he currently has a peon at his office. And when my father found out that the peon had just become a parent for the second time, he asked the peon about his goals. The peon stressed how much he wanted to give his girls an education and a life. Nevertheless, he was worried about the family finances all the time. My father suggested that he buy a battery-powered tricycle so that he could use it to generate an additional income from the allowance because he could not be given a salary increment. The peon followed his recommendation, and he was now in a position to make his children's future financially secure after managing to lease an electric rickshaw in the morning, besides that, he operates a self-driving rickshaw in the evening after work. The help my father gave was not only in terms of money, but it was more than that, which positively changed the life of the peon to achieve the desired goal.

Being thankful was the last core value that my dad lived by. He said that being thankful was the key to happiness and that recognising and accepting the good things in life opened the door to even more good things. No matter how small, he always looked for the good in things.

He taught me how to be thankful, and he always told me that there is no such thing as a perfect time. We just have to make the time we have now beautiful.

The Lasting Impact of Character and Personal Growth

In this way, it's easy for me to see that my father's greatest gift wasn't what he said, did, or accomplished, but what kind of person he became. A phrase he liked to use was "What we possess is temporary; what we germinate is permanent." This idea guided him in everything he did, whether it was dealing with his own problems or helping other people solve theirs.

My father's life was a clear example of his morals, his drive to get better, and his moral traits. He said that he had never thought that success meant having a lot of money, a great job, or any other kind of material or professional satisfaction. Instead, he thought that success meant making a difference in people's lives. He showed this belief in every part of his life, from the little things he did, like the random acts of kindness, to the big things he did, like donating organs, paying for his peers' kids to go to school, or planning their best future.

It was clear to me that my dad is dedicated to helping others and growing. He would pay for his housekeeper's child to go to school, give money for his driver's heart surgery, or just give someone words of support. He lived a life that showed me how to be persistent, grateful, and generous, and these lessons have stuck with me deeply.

Even though all of the events in my father's life story involve danger and trouble, the lessons he taught me are easy to understand. His stories turned into not only stories of survival but also stories of beating bad news with unshakeable hope, even when he fell off a terrace, wasn't around when a fire called for him, or was even hit by someone else. As for me, these negative pictures helped me understand that tough times don't make people weak; they make them stronger.

These events have taught us that sadness is a part of life and that how we deal with it makes us who we are! Dad taught me that dealing with and overcoming issues is what makes you happy and gives you hope, not having them. This lesson is about fighting through hard times with hope and bravery. First, we need to understand that troubles are a part of life, but they shouldn't control our actions or choices. Problems shouldn't stop us from becoming better people and getting things done. Instead, they should help us become more productive humans. This faith showed in the way he lived his life, and I made sure to do the same in mine. When I do the things he taught me, I always remember that happiness is the way—the way to figure out who we are, the way to keep going, and the way to help other people. How many lives we can change with our success is what my dad told me. Success isn't about who we are or what we have. This person set an excellent example for me, and I want to remember them as well

The Journey Continues

Encouragement the journey of happiness

I feel thankful and inspired when I think about what my dad has taught me and how I can find happiness. In his book "**Happiness: How, When, and Why**"- these three words have always helped me get through tough times. By watching what my father did and said, I was lucky enough to gain a lot of knowledge that changed how I think about happiness, persistence, and purpose. He often quoted Aristotle, who said, "Knowing yourself is the beginning of all wisdom." This was one of the most important things he taught me. This idea pushed me to think about myself and make decisions that were in line with my virtues. Another important lesson was dealing with setbacks. A Japanese saying that helped me remember this was "Fall seven times, stand up eight." I learnt from this that failure is not the end, but the first step towards victory. My dad also learnt to be grateful. He told me, "Gratitude turns what we have into enough," and he made sure I had a good attitude about life. He thought a lot about spirituality, and at the start of his course, he quoted Lord Krishna from the Bhagavad Gita: "Yoga is the journey of the self, through the self, to the self." Getting more spiritually aware helped me understand what real happiness is. I have promised to follow these rules as I continue on this road to honour his memory. I like the three words "**Engage, Retain, Grow**," because they sum up what he taught me and how I should live my life. To keep people happy, I think it's important to remember these beliefs. Others can be encouraged to do the same.